SYSTEMATIC SELLING

TERRY A. MORT

SYSTEMATIC SELLING

HOW TO INFLUENCE
THE BUYING DECISION PROCESS

amacom

A DIVISION OF AMERICAN MANAGEMENT ASSOCIATIONS

Library of Congress Cataloging in Publication Data
Mort, Terry A
    Systematic selling.

    Includes index.
    1. Selling. 2. Purchasing. I. Title.
HF5438.25.M67   658.85   77-5937
ISBN 0-8144-5439-9

First Printing

TO MY FATHER, E. V. MORT

CONTENTS

INTRODUCTION

Along Route 22 in eastern Pennsylvania there is a motel well past its prime. It has 10 or 12 cottages clustered around a slightly larger house that serves as the office, and all of these could use a coat of paint. Competition is fairly stiff in that area, and this motel has had to contend with the modern chains and their signs proclaiming POOL, SAUNA, IN-ROOM MOVIES, RESTAURANT, LOUNGE, and so on. The small motel had none of these attractions. Nonetheless, it responded to the competition by putting up a sign of its own, one which advertised its own unique benefit. If you are driving that way, you can still see the sign and its proud message: STEAM HEAT.

That motel has always seemed to me a good symbol of the way many salesmen sell. They concentrate on telling their prospective customers about whatever unique features and benefits their product has. Our motel didn't have much to offer, but it did have steam heat, and the owner was going to let the world know. He didn't stop to think that most people don't care what kind of heat a motel has. Nor did he consider that in the summer, that sign would not appeal to travelers who'd spent the day in a hot car. His concern was to find a competitive edge, and he turned to his *product* for it.

Unfortunately, unique feature or not, the world simply didn't care about steam heat. Consequently the place needs a coat of paint, this year even more than last.

Salesmen often run into a similar problem, and it generally stems from mistaking the act of talking about a product for the process of selling it. Certainly, being able to describe a product—to advertise its features, unique and otherwise—is an important aspect of selling, but it is only one aspect, and it often comes quite late in the process. Other elements, which precede the "presentation," are concerned with uncovering and analyzing the prospect's requirements so that the eventual presentation will be a response tailored to the individual situation rather than an abrupt shotgun proclamation of product benefits. Anybody going around announcing "steam heat" will make a sale only if he encounters someone who is concerned about heating methods. On the other hand, the salesman who first investigates his prospect's goals and needs will be in a position to present an effective outline of how his product meets those criteria better than the competition. It may well be, for instance, that many travelers are most concerned with the cost of the rooms, in which case our small motel would have a genuine edge over the higher-priced competition. But you would never know that if you did not first analyze your prospect's situation. If you neglect to do that analysis, you are not selling. All you are doing is putting up signs.

If selling is not simply describing a product, what is it? What are the basic elements of the sales process? Just how *do* you analyze a prospect's situation so that you can make an effective presentation?

The answers to these questions are based on a simple fact: Buying is decision making. Selling, therefore, is developing buying decisions.

People buy something because they have decided to do so. If they do not buy, it is because they have decided that the choices available to them do not measure up to their criteria. Salesmen cannot decide for their customers; their job is to *engineer* their buying decisions.

Part of the salesman's problem stems from the fact that there is no universally agreed-upon method which people follow when making decisions—whether they be buying decisions or any other kind. Some buy impulsively. Others spend hours agonizing over endless bits of data before acting. Still others organize available information carefully and evaluate products systematically. The salesman, in other words, must deal with all kinds of decision makers—the fast, the slow, the analytical, the subjective.

Salesmen must be concerned with the *quality* of the buying decision. Because they generally live on repeat business, it is important to them that their customers make good decisions, decisions that accurately reflect their needs and limitations. Everyone has heard the story of the super salesman who could sell iceboxes to Eskimos. But no one ever says what happened after the Eskimos had a chance to think about their purchase. How likely is it that that salesman could sell them anything on his next trip?

The salesman's problem is to develop quality buying decisions with customers who very often would not make good choices if left to their own devices. On the other hand, he naturally must try to engineer the buyer's decisions in a way that helps him sell his product. In order to achieve these two key objectives, the salesman needs to understand how decisions are made—or should be made. He needs a model of the ideal, systematic decision-making process that he can overlay onto the often haphazard decision methods of his customers. That model becomes the basis of his interaction with the prospect. The prospect remains the decision maker, but the salesman is his guide through the process.

For example, a buyer for a chemical company was asked what he was looking for in salesmen who called on him. His answer was: "I want to deal with a salesman who knows us down to our underwear." Notice he said "knows us," not "knows his product." Product knowledge is taken for granted. What this buyer wanted was a salesman who could, in a way, act as a consultant—someone who was willing to get to know his problems, objectives, and plans and who in this way would enable him to make the best use of the salesman's products and expertise. He wanted someone, in other words, who would help him make the best possible decisions.

The salesman's problem, in short, is to develop buying decisions that will benefit both his customers and his own company. In order to accomplish that task, however, he must first gain an understanding of the ideal buying-decision process. If he's going to engineer a good buying decision, he needs to know what one is.

ONE

SYSTEMATIC BUYING

Forget for the moment that your job is to sell. Instead, concentrate on another activity that you also perform much of your time and that you constantly encounter: buying.

Most people would agree that there are two basic elements in any decision to buy: the ends and the means—the things I as a buyer want and the choices available to satisfy those wants. The key to a good decision is the order in which those two elements— ends and means—are considered: In a good buying decision, the ends are precisely identified *before* the means are evaluated.

The reason why this sequence is so important is that most decisions are compromises. The products and services among which we have to choose generally fall short of the ideal. How many people, for instance, can honestly say they live in a house that suits them perfectly in every respect? Anyone who has built or bought a house—or, for that matter, rented an apartment—knows that at some point he had to strike a compromise between what he had in mind and what was realistically available to him.

Generally these compromises are dictated by budget limitations, but very commonly they may also be the results of limited supplies. Anyone who experienced the shortages in 1973 and 1974 probably remembers that some industrial buyers had to settle for far smaller shipments of raw materials than they wanted (and could pay for) simply because there was not enough supply. In some cases they had to settle for substitute materials.

Whether in consumer goods, industrial products, or personal services, the buyer almost always compromises with his ideal. There are always limitations that must be endured.

Good buying, therefore, is a matter of choosing the *best available,* rather than the perfect, product or service; perfection generally does not exist. To put it another way, good buying is making the least possible compromise with perfection.

This is why following the proper sequence of the steps in the decision-making process is so important. By first precisely identifying my goals, the ends that I want to achieve with my purchase, I am establishing a set of criteria against which to measure the variously flawed choices I have available. If I don't first consider what I want in a house, how can I evaluate the colonial in the country against the town house in the city or the split-level in the suburbs? None of them is perfect, so which of them is best? I have no way of knowing unless I first define exactly what it is I am looking for. Only then can I measure how well each alternative performs.

That may seem awfully simple, but consider the way most people make buying decisions. They rarely know precisely what they want before they begin to mull over their choices. If they did, the term "impulse buying" would not be a part of the English language.

Good decision making is a controlled *process*—a logical series of steps arranged in a sequence that will yield predictable results when followed. In paper-making, cut logs are fed into one end of the mill and huge rolls of finished paper emerge from the other. To get from the first stage to the last, the wood must be processed in a series of steps, and each step has a well-defined specific function. If any of them is omitted or the sequence of the steps altered, the final product will be unsatisfactory.

The same is true of the decision process. There are certain essential steps through which the buyer should go, and they are arranged in a sequence that he should observe. Overlooking or rearranging any of these steps is almost sure to result in a poor buying decision.

As we have said, the two basic elements in any buying decision are the ends to be achieved and the means available to you. The sequence in which they are considered is crucial: You cannot effectively evaluate your choices *before* establishing your criteria. More specifically, to make a quality buying decision you must go through the following steps:

A. Defining the ends
  1. *Establishing the need for action.* Ask yourself if a decision is *necessary* at all. There are only three valid motives for considering action:
    (a) You have become aware of an *opportunity* to improve your current situation, satisfactory though that situation may be.
    (b) You are *dissatisfied* with your current situation.

7

SYSTEMATIC SELLING

(c) You perceive a *risk* that your current satisfactory situation may deteriorate.

2. *Identifying the basic goal.* What is your decision all about? What are you trying to achieve? Make sure that you haven't adopted too broad or too narrow a goal definition.

3. *Defining the criteria for evaluating the alternatives.* This involves three questions that should be answered in the order in which they are listed here:

(a) What inflexible *constraints* are there that limit your choices from the start?

(b) What desirable, but not altogether inflexible, *objectives* do you want to achieve with your decision?

(c) What are the *priorities* of these objectives? How important is each one to you?

B. Evaluating the means

1. *Determining compatibility of the available means with your constraints.* Do any of the alternatives under consideration not meet your constraints? If so, eliminate those choices.

2. *Evaluating inherent risks.* Are there any unacceptable risks attached to any of the alternatives? If yes, eliminate the choices in question.

3. *Evaluating the alternatives in the light of the objectives.* How does each alternative perform against each of the objectives, starting with the most important objective and working down?

4. *Weighing the overall performance of the alternatives.* Which of the choices available to

8

you provides the best cumulative performance against your priority-ranked list of objectives? The answer to this last question singles out the product or service that is your best choice. It probably falls short of perfection, but it represents the least possible compromise with it.

The remainder of this chapter will be devoted to a more detailed discussion of these steps constituting the systematic buying process.

Defining the Ends

Establishing the Need for Action

The first step in the buying-decision process is to consider whether action is at all necessary. In other words, you should question your motives for even entering the decision-making process. We are not yet talking about the motivation to *buy* a particular product, but only about reasons to *consider buying;* you may be well-motivated to consider a group of products and ultimately decide not to buy. It is important to remember this distinction.

There are only three rational motives for entering the buying-decision process:

- Because you see an *opportunity* to improve an already satisfactory situation.
- Because you are *dissatisfied* with your current situation.
- Because you perceive a *risk* that your current situation may deteriorate if you do not take action.

Opportunity for improvement. When an investor learns about a particularly attractive new stock, he sees an opportunity to improve his portfolio. When a purchasing agent learns of a price cut in a commodity, he sees an opportunity to improve his company's supply situation. In neither case is the buyer committed at this stage, but he is motivated to enter the decision process, to begin looking at the product and evaluating its compatibility with his own goals, needs, and limitations. This evaluation may show that the new stock is unsuited to the investor's situation or that the lower-priced commodity does not meet the purchasing agent's quality standards. The point is that in each case the potential buyer is motivated to consider a possible purchase because he sees a chance to improve his situation, satisfactory though it may be.

Dissatisfaction. Unlike the person who considers a purchase in order to improve a satisfactory situation, the dissatisfied prospect has a strong built-in motivation to enter the decision process insofar as he can see that doing so might lead to alleviation of his troubled state.

You may be dissatisfied with a previous buying decision or with the general situation. In either case, you obviously would be interested in evaluating a possible purchase that might rectify the unsatisfactory situation. There *is* one important difference between the two situations, however: If you're dissatisfied with a previous buying decision, you are a poor prospect for the salesman who engineered it—and a very good one for his competitors.

To introduce some examples from industrial selling, consider a plant manager who is dissatisfied with some aspect of his operation. No external motive— say, an attractive opportunity to increase the efficiency of the plant operations in unforeseen ways— has to be supplied to this person; he already has a good internal motive to consider a new product or service that could bring plant performance up to expectations. On the other hand, consider the situation of the purchasing agent, in the same company, who bought a product that the plant manager found deficient in some way. No doubt the purchasing agent will hear about it soon. He too will have a good motive to look around for a new product; but he's unlikely to buy it from the salesman who sold him the original unsatisfactory product. He is an excellent prospect for the competition.

Perceived risk. A prospect will be motivated to consider a purchase if he sees that by not taking action he might bring about a deterioration of his present situation and if he feels that a particular product or service would eliminate or reduce the risk.

Insurance salesmen have traditionally motivated their prospects to listen to them by pointing out the risks they face if they do not consider ways to protect themselves and their families. It can be pretty grim stuff to the prospect, and insurance people have lately added the additional motivation of opportunity, for instance, by pointing out the investment potential of various insurance programs. Even without this extra motive, however, the risk to the family finances is usually real enough to warrant at least consideration of the insurance product.

All too often insurance salesmen mistake motivating the prospect to begin the decision process with motivating him to buy. They stop at pointing out various risks, and while they may have persuaded the prospect to analyze the way certain insurance programs might fit his personal situation, he is by no means ready to sign an application. He is motivated to enter the decision process, but he is certainly not ready to buy.

A key point that will occupy us through much of

this book is that these motives for considering action are only as strong as the prospect's *perception* of them. A risk, however real, will not motivate a person to act unless he sees it clearly. An opportunity, however marvelous, will not galvanize a buyer into action unless he is aware of it. Once he perceives that he has a valid motive, he can then decide how best to deal with it.

To look at things from the salesman's point of view for a moment: Why do we have to worry about motivation at all? What difference does it make *why* a person enters the buying-decision process? Isn't it enough to know that the prospect *is* in fact ready to evaluate the market?

The answer is: Motives do make a difference. As we've just said, a motive is only as strong as the prospect's perception of it, and the stronger the motive, the greater the likelihood of an eventual purchase. Hence, in order to start the buyer on the decision process, the salesman must sharpen the buyer's perception of his own motives. Understanding the three basic types of motives for considering action tells the salesman where to look, on which aspects of the buyer's situation to concentrate.

People are naturally reluctant to make decisions, and with good reason: Any change in their situation carries the seeds of new problems. The salesman cannot overcome this natural inertia unless he can convince the prospect that he should be dissatisfied with his current situation or that either an unacceptable risk or an attractive opportunity calls for action on his part.

For example, put yourself in the position of a purchasing agent who has dealt with a supplier over a number of years and consistently experienced prompt deliveries, reasonable prices, continuity of supplies, and good service. In short, he has been and continues to be satisfied with the supplier. There are only three conditions under which he should even consider buying from someone else: if he sees an opportunity to improve his already satisfactory situation, if he becomes aware of a risk that the situation could deteriorate, or if the previously satisfactory relationship with the supplier suddenly becomes unsatisfactory. In the absence of any such motive the purchasing agent would be unwise to reconsider his original decision, because by switching to another supplier he would only open himself up to potential problems that do not now exist.

Looking at the situation from the point of view of the two salesmen—the one who currently has the account and his competitor—we can see that both need to understand the purchasing agent's basic motives for considering a change. The first salesman must make certain to keep the purchasing agent satisfied, that is, to give him no motive for reconsidering his decision. The other salesman has to probe for possible dissatisfactions with the current supplier, present the purchasing agent with an attractive opportunity (for instance, a significant price reduction or new technology) or point out a risk (upcoming shortages, a strike at the present supplier's). If he cannot identify a specific item within these three categories of motivation, he will not get past the first interview.

In summary, then, understanding what motivates people to consider taking action helps the salesman start the prospect on the decision process. For the buyer, on the other hand, an understanding of these motives is necessary in order to determine at the outset whether it is worthwhile to consider a purchase.

Identifying the Basic Goal

Once the decision maker has determined that action is indeed called for, his next step should be to make sure that he understands clearly what he is trying to achieve.

To use a simple example, suppose you have a long steep driveway that is impassable after an inch or so of snow. After being snowed in three or four times and perhaps missing business opportunities because of it, you throw up your hands in exasperation and declare you won't spend another day without a four-wheel-drive vehicle that can get you up and down that driveway no matter how bad the snow. Your problem, apparently, is which four-wheel-drive vehicle to buy.

But is it? What are you really trying to do? You want to make sure you can get up your driveway in any weather. Your problem, therefore, is to select the best means to do that. A four-wheel-drive vehicle is one solution, but to narrow the decision to that possibility means to neglect whole groups of alternatives—for instance, buying a snowblower or snowmobile or hiring a snow removal service—which might achieve your true goal more efficiently. To make an optimal choice, then, it is essential to define precisely what one wants to accomplish.

To use a more technical example, engineers in charge of public drinking water systems often have to contend with corrosion problems in the system's pipes. These pipes are generally made of cast iron. In time the metal will blister, and small pieces will break off into the water and discolor it. The more acidic the water, the greater the corrosion problem. The traditional remedy, therefore, has been to adjust the pH of the water by adding caustic soda (a base) to the water. This reduces the acidity and thereby the corrosion in the pipes. For years, then, the engineers of these water systems have defined their problem as that of selecting the best supplier of caustic soda.

But that definition does not accurately reflect what they were really trying to do. Their basic goal was to eliminate corrosion in the pipes. Adding caustic soda represents one method of adjusting the pH, and adjusting the pH is a way of reducing corrosion. There are others, however, for instance, using certain chemicals to seal off the metal and thereby insulate it from the water. If that solution is adopted, the metal is protected from corrosion no matter how acidic the water.

Because the engineers mistakenly defined their basic goal as that of choosing the best caustic soda supplier, they may have cut themselves off from cheaper, more effective, and safer ways of dealing with the corrosion problem in water pipes.

Defining your primary goal is, in a sense, setting the basic boundaries that will constrain your decision. The term is useful in that it describes graphically what the decision maker is doing at this stage: He is drawing a boundary around the choices that he can make and excluding all others. In our water treatment example, the narrower goal definition set the basic boundary so as to exclude all alternatives except the suppliers of caustic soda. Because of this narrow boundary, all other possible methods of dealing with the corrosion problem received no attention.

If the goal definition were broadened, however, to read *to decide on the best means to reduce corrosion,* a great many new alternative methods could be considered. While the caustic soda alternative is not eliminated, others are now included, and it seems clear that the more choices available, the greater the possibility of finding one that closely matches the buyer's ideal.

The basic goal, then, acts like a boundary because

it directs the decision maker's attention to one group of alternatives and excludes all others.

Identification of the primary objective is a key step in the decision process. On the one hand, it can improve the quality of the decision, as in our water treatment example; on the other, it can make the process more efficient, because it eliminates irrelevant alternatives and focuses the attention where it belongs. To illustrate our point about efficiency, consider the situation of an executive who is transferred to the New York area. Suppose this executive has lived in the area before and knows that he wants to reside in Connecticut and commute to the city. His basic goal, then, would be to select a house in Connecticut within commuting distance of the city. By setting the boundaries of his decision so narrowly he avoids having to evaluate houses in New Jersey, Long Island, Westchester County, and many other areas, and therefore saves valuable time and energy. Someone unfamiliar with the area, on the other hand, would of course be wise to settle for the less specific goal of choosing a house within commuting distance of New York City, in which case all suburban alternatives would have to be considered.

In short, having a clear idea of your primary objective is the basic prerequisite for recognizing the relevant alternatives and reaching an efficient yet optimal decision.

From the salesman's point of view, as we will see in more detail in later chapters, understanding how the buyer's basic goal influences his choice is a key factor in shaping the buying decision. Competing chemical salesmen, for example, would want the water treatment engineers to define their problem quite differently. If you were a caustic soda salesman, you would be content to have the primary objective identified as the selection of the best way to adjust the pH; actually you would prefer the even narrower goal of choosing the best supplier of caustic soda. Your competitor, on the other hand, who sells a chemical that coats the pipes without affecting the pH, would want the engineers to adopt the expanded goal of finding the best method to reduce corrosion, because this would allow his product to get into the race.

Defining Criteria for Evaluating the Alternatives

Once the buyer has defined exactly what he is trying to accomplish with his decision, his next step is to set the criteria against which he can measure the various alternatives. We said earlier that any decision represents a compromise of some degree. Because of this, it is essential to establish the criteria you will be using before you begin to evaluate your choices; otherwise you have no way of telling which of your alternatives is the best.

These evaluation criteria further refine what the decision maker is trying to achieve. They represent a complete description of the buyer's *ideal choice*. Although this ideal does not really exist, it nonetheless is the only standard against which the real-world alternatives can be measured. To know which choice comes closest to your ideal, you obviously must have a clear concept of the latter.

An important benefit of carefully selecting your ideal criteria is that you as the buyer will understand the exact nature of your compromise—and generally your buying decision will be a compromise. The more precisely you know why and to what degree you have made a compromise, the less likely you will be later to feel dissatisfied with your choice. To put it differently, if, knowing in advance that certain aspects of your ideal will not be matched, you decide on a product that meets a realistic maximum of important criteria, you will be unlikely to dwell on these deficiencies later. For instance, if I know at the time of purchase that my car will not get 25 miles per gallon, I will probably not be upset at the mileage after I've driven it for a while. By contrast, if I do not consider this mileage criterion at all *before* buying the car, I am likely to be surprised and unhappy. And even though I have no one to blame but myself, the salesman who engineered my decision will be a joint target—along with the car itself—of my dissatisfaction.

In short, the point of these remarks is that prior to evaluating the alternatives available to him, the decision maker must set his criteria carefully; as a statement of the ideal choice, they are the only yardstick against which to measure the actual choices. Evaluation criteria fall into three categories: constraints, objectives, and priorities.

Constraints. If there were no such things as budgets, delivery schedules, inventory limitations, or manpower restrictions, the lives of buyers and salesmen would be greatly simplified. Unfortunately, that is not the case. Customers always must observe certain limitations when making a buying decision. There are always factors acting upon the decision maker and restricting the range of his decision. These are the buyer's constraints.

Budget constraints are the most obvious example. Whether the buyer is a purchasing agent for a multinational corporation or a brand-new father considering an insurance policy, there is always a ceiling on what he can spend. As Mr. Micawber said in *David Copperfield:* "Income 20 pounds, expenses 19 pounds, 19 shillings, 6 pence—happiness. Income 20 pounds, expenses 20 pounds, 1 shilling—misery."

By definition, constraints are inflexible. If a buyer

has only so much money to spend, that limit cannot be exceeded. If a warehouse has only so much inventory capacity, it cannot purchase in excess of that capacity. If a mill runs on an inflexible production schedule, suppliers must meet that schedule. There are no arguments about constraints. They are rigid; if a product or service does not meet them, it cannot be considered, no matter how appealing its other features may be.

Constraints act not unlike the basic goal. Just as the latter focuses the buyer's attention on one group of choices to the exclusion of all others, so does a constraint. If my basic goal is the purchase of a car and my budget is $5,000, that constraint automatically eliminates all cars costing more, narrowing my focus on those cars that fall within my budget limit.

There are a number of common sources of constraints. Money, as we have said, is the most obvious. Time—for instance, rigid schedules that must be met—is another. Space is a third. Manpower availability is another; for example, an industrial buyer cannot consider equipment that requires more manpower for its operation than he has at his disposal. In short, constraints are derived from *resources*, for resources, whether money, men, or materials, are always limited.

To exceed a genuine constraint would generally have disastrous consequences for the buyer. Hence it is important that he state all constraints as precisely as possible, for if he is too general, it will be hard to determine whether a particular product falls within his limits. For instance, it is perfectly easy to determine whether a particular car costs $5,000 or less. If, on the other hand, the buyer had adopted a less specific constraint, such as "reasonable cost," he would have had a much more difficult time evaluating various cars in the light of his budget. What is reasonable in one case may be exorbitant in another, but $5,000 is always $5,000.

An important point about constraints is that they should be kept to a minimum. There is an element of judgment involved here, and decision makers sometimes show a tendency to impose more restrictions on their choices than necessary. The more constraints there are, the narrower the decision maker's focus, and hence the fewer the alternatives among which to choose. Keeping constraints to a minimum keeps the decision maker's range of alternatives as broad as possible.

In short, the decision maker should consider as constraints only those factors which are truly inflexible. The fewer and the more precisely stated, the better.

Objectives. While constraints are, in a sense, negative criteria, separating the products the buyer can consider from those he cannot, objectives are positive. They represent the things the buyer wants to achieve as a result of his purchase.

Whereas constraints should be kept to a minimum, objectives can and should be extensive. The buyer's ultimate goal is to choose the best possible product or service; the more objectives he can identify, the more adequate a tool he will have for evaluating the available alternatives. Suppose, for instance, that you are looking for a car and have established a budget constraint of $5,000. If you decided that your only objective was to have a four-door car, you would be hard put to make a choice among all the eligible alternatives. By contrast, suppose you compiled an extensive list of objectives, say:

Lowest cost
20 MPG
Four doors

Automatic transmission
Vinyl top
AM/FM radio
Air conditioning
Neutral color
Six-cylinder motor

Having a complete picture of your "ideal" car, you would now be able to measure existing alternatives against it. You are, in short, creating a blueprint of the car you want, and your decision becomes a matter of ascertaining which available model comes closest to your design specifications.

Another important characteristic of objectives is that unlike constraints, they are not inflexible. Constraints are all equally important: They are inviolable. By contrast, objectives vary in importance; some are more flexible, some less. To put it differently, they can be ranked according to priority.

Constraints are the inflexible limits within which I must work; objectives represent the desired results of my purchase. Knowing that the alternatives I have available will all call for some sort of compromise, I know in advance that some of my objectives will not be met or met less fully than I would ideally want. In short, objectives are my area of compromise.

Priorities. The combined list of constraints and objectives describes your ideal choice. If products and services could meet that ideal, setting priorities among your objectives would be unnecessary. But since a purchase generally represents a compromise with the ideal, objectives must be ranked according to importance. If I have to compromise, let it be in areas of low importance. If I have to sacrifice certain objectives altogether, let it be those which mean the least to me. In short, I need to know what my priorities are.

As we have seen, only objectives can be prioritized. Constraints are inflexible and as such are all of equal importance.

Unfortunately, there is no simple formula telling the decision maker *how* to set priorities; intelligent judgment is required for this. The model of the systematic buying decision process that we are discussing shows you that you need to order your objectives according to relative importance, but it can't *do* it for you. As we shall see, however, it is in this area that the salesman can contribute significantly to the buying decision.

EVALUATING THE MEANS

Let us briefly review the situation of the buyer who has followed the decision-making process to this point. First he established that some kind of action was in fact necessary and identified his basic goal. Those two steps completed, he defined his evaluation criteria, starting with the inflexible constraints that the product of his choice must meet, going on to his more flexible objectives, and finishing with the order of importance of the objectives. In short, he has constructed an image of his ideal choice. Having thus defined his ends, the decision maker now has a complete set of criteria for evaluating the alternatives available to him.

Checking for Compatibility with Constraints

Evaluating choices as to their compatibility with the constraints that you established in the first phase of the decision process should not involve relative judgments. If you have defined your constraints clearly and kept them specific, evaluation will yield a simple yes or no. For instance, a house either meets a $50,000 budget constraint or it doesn't; there isn't any in-between.

It might be suggested that a $40,000 house meets a $50,000 budget constraint "better" than a $49,000 one, but that is an incorrect view: There is no difference at all between the two as far as the budget *constraint* is concerned; rather, the cheaper house performs better than the other one against an additional *objective*, namely "lowest cost." It would be wrong to introduce such an objective at this early stage of the evaluation process. Objectives, as we have seen, are flexible and do not eliminate choices in any simple way. They need to be "put in perspective," or prioritized, before they can fruitfully bear on the decision.

At this point, then, the decision maker must examine each alternative and ask a simple question: Does it meet all my constraints? If so, it can be considered further; if not, it must be dropped.

Evaluating Inherent Risks

The next step in the evaluation process is to ask, for each alternative, whether there are any unacceptable risks attached to it. As with constraints, consideration of risks serves to eliminate alternatives from consideration, and the clearer the buyer's idea of what constitutes an unacceptable risk to him, the more efficient the elimination process.

Risks are inherent in the choices, and for that reason they cannot well be considered in advance, before the alternatives are examined in detail. To put it differently, evaluating risks means asking questions like "Suppose I choose supplier A. Given what I know about A, what unacceptable risks might I be running?" The answer to that question obviously must be postponed until I am ready to take a close look at supplier A.

There will undoubtedly be times when a buyer is uncertain whether a risk exists, or if so, whether he would be willing to accept it. In such a case he might want to delay the decision until he is able to quantify the extent of the risk and determine the advisability of accepting it. If he is still unsure, he has the final option of adding a "risk avoidance objective" to his list of evaluation criteria. This objective would then serve as an additional test that any product must pass in order to be selected.

Matching Alternatives against Objectives

The next task is to consider each objective *singly* and to compare how closely each alternative comes to meeting it. Since this is done objective by objective, it is natural and useful to proceed according to the priority list, that is, to consider objectives in descending order of importance. This leads us to the next and last step.

Weighing the Alternatives' Comparative Merits

The point of establishing firm priorities is to avoid unnecessary and unproductive confusion. It is usually true that different alternatives do different things well. One car, for instance, may give you good mileage while another offers more riding comfort. If you haven't clearly defined your priorities, you may never come to a decision or leave it to the dice.

Your last step, then, is to determine which of the alternatives provides the best performance against your top-rated objectives. This will be your best choice, representing the least compromise with your ideal.

SUMMARY

In review, a systematic buying decision can be reconstructed as a process in which I answer a series of questions:

What are my ends?
> Do I need to act at all?
> - Is there a worthwhile *opportunity* to improve my situation?
> - Am I or should I be *dissatisfied* with current circumstances?
> - Is there a *risk* that the situation might deteriorate unless I take action?
>
> What is my *basic goal?* What am I really trying to achieve?
>
> What *criteria* shall I use to evaluate the available alternatives?
> - What are the genuine inflexible *constraints* limiting the range of my choice?
> - What are the *objectives* that I would like to achieve as a result of my decision?
> - What is the order of *priority* of my objectives?

How well do the available means match these ends?
> - Are there any alternatives that fail to meet one of my *constraints?* They cannot be considered further.
> - Are there any *unacceptable risks* attached to any alternative? Again, this disqualifies the choice in question.
> - How well does each alternative meet each of my *objectives?*
> - Which of the alternatives meets most of my *important* objectives best? This is my optimal choice.

TWO

A BRIEF CASE STUDY

It will be useful at this point to illustrate the steps involved in the systematic buying process with a hypothetical case. As you read the following, put yourself in the position of the purchasing agent at the Archer Metals Company and decide, using our model of the rational buying decision, which company he should choose as supplier.

THE BUYER: ARCHER METALS COMPANY

Archer Metals Company, a large steel and aluminum distributor on the East Coast, has been in business fifty years and has grown steadily to the point of $30 million annual sales. Its primary business consists of buying various types of steel and aluminum from producers and warehousing and marketing it to a variety of end users.

Archer has six warehouses—two in Pennsylvania, two in North Carolina, and one each in South Carolina and New York. At each location there is a sales staff consisting of inside phone salesmen and outside direct salesmen.

Archer's products are aluminum plates and sheets, carbon-steel tubing and pipes, and stainless steel in all forms. While the company does offer certain limited fabricating services, its success has primarily been the result of intelligent buying and inventory control. It has been, in other words, a straightforward warehouse operation.

Recently, however, Archer sought and won a contract with Fowler Office Furniture to supply Fowler with stainless-steel legs for their desks and desk chairs. The contract calls for Archer to deliver chair legs which have been cut, polished, and bent according to Fowler's specifications. Fowler will then assemble these legs directly to its desks and chairs without further fabrication.

For Archer, this contract means a radical departure from its traditional business since it will involve not only buying the basic stainless steel tubes but also converting them into finished furniture legs. The problem now is to select a supplier for the steel tubing. Archer considered the possibility of buying its own tube mill and manufacturing the tubes in its Philadelphia plant, but abandoned this idea because of the cost of the necessary equipment.

All cutting and bending will be done at Archer's main location in Philadelphia. Since most tubing is priced exclusive of delivery costs, Archer would be able to realize some savings by selecting a supplier in the local area. The company could then use its own trucks to pick up the tubes and thereby avoid freight charges.

Archer's contract with Fowler calls for regular delivery of the various pieces each month for the next year. This means that Archer will need to buy its tubing on an equally regular basis throughout the year, because its available inventory space is not sufficient to hold enough tubing to last the term of the contract. It is crucial, therefore, that any supplier Archer deals with be able to meet this delivery schedule. Slowdowns in production could seriously jeopardize the contract with Fowler. All the major producers of tubing have sufficient production capacity to meet Archer's schedule, but there is a potential problem with their sources of supply. Tube manufacturers buy the steel from which they make tubing from the large steel producers. They are dependent on these suppliers, and in times of shortage the big steel companies put the tube manufacturers on allocation.

The supply situation is very hazy at the moment, and there is real concern at Archer to select a tube manufacturer with a sufficient allocation of basic metal. There is similar concern at Fowler—so much so that it has stipulated as part of the contract that Archer must use a tube supplier that has a guaranteed source of basic steel.

Although most producers of tubing have fairly similar prices, Archer believes that since it is buying such a massive amount of tubing (600,000 feet over the year), the tube manufacturers can afford to cut their prices. Archer has budgeted $500,000 for tubing and is determined to stay within that figure. To exceed that amount would mean taking a loss on the Fowler contract because of initial heavy outlays for the cutting and bending equipment.

Because of its strict budget, Archer is willing to sign an exclusive contract with a supplier, expecting that this will further induce the tube manufacturers to cut their prices. While it makes Archer a little nervous to be restricted to one supplier, especially since regular supply is crucial, the company is willing to do so in order to meet the budget and not to have to worry about price hikes down the road. Additionally, as Archer's vice president of finance puts it: "Just because we're budgeted at $500,000 doesn't mean we'll be unhappy if we don't spend it all."

The quality of the tubing is of great importance since it will be made into furniture legs, which must be decorative as well as strong. Archer of course realizes that some tubes will be damaged during shipment, and it has budgeted for such losses. But the allowance for damage is just 1 percent; anything beyond that is a serious quality problem. Archer wants to deal with a company, therefore, that can meet its quality standard and will provide continuous technical assistance should quality problems occur. Since this is Archer's first foray into tube fabrication, it would prefer to use a supplier that would be able to offer the company a broad range of technical services if this should be required.

A related concern is the quality of the tube finish. All manufacturers offer to polish their tubing, but the quality of the finish varies from company to company. Needless to say, for the decorative desk and chair legs that Fowler wants, the polish would have to be mirror finish.

Another factor about which Archer is concerned is the method by which the tubing is made. Stainless tubes are generally formed by subjecting lengths of flat steel to a series of bending operations. The bending gradually forces the long sides of the steel up and around until they meet, thus forming the tube. The two sides are then welded together.

It is this welding operation that concerns Archer. There are two kinds of welding mills: high-frequency and TIG (tungsten inert gas). The high-frequency method is fast—four times faster than the TIG welding method. The TIG weld, however, provides a better bond. The quality of the bond is important to Archer because it will be bending some of the tubing, especially that for the chair legs, and if high-frequency welding is used, the bending will occasionally cause separation of the weld. This problem does not occur in TIG-welded tubes.

Archer is preparing its cutting and bending production line and estimates that it will be ready in ninety days. The first shipment of 100,000 feet of tubing should therefore be in Archer's hands by that time.

Finally, Archer is mildly worried about dealing with a non-union shop. The company is experiencing some labor unrest, and management feels that it would be best to deal with a tube manufacturer that is unionized. Archer believes that dealing with a non-union company might antagonize its already touchy employees.

There are only four manufacturers of stainless tubing that are large enough to be worth considering: Ames Steel Tube, Zenith Tube, Hazleton Products, and Futura Steel.

CHOICE 1: AMES STEEL TUBE

A representative of Ames Steel Tube of Pittsburgh has been especially aggressive in seeking the contract with Archer. This aggressiveness may be related to strong and fairly reliable rumors that Ames's parent, Cosmo Steel, is going to sell or close down the subsidiary within a year unless its profit picture improves. The salesman from Ames has no information on the rumor.

At any rate, Ames is offering a contract price of $450,000 to produce the entire 600,000 feet. Because it is owned by a major steel producer, there will be no trouble about getting the steel that it will need to produce the tubes. It has continuous access to Cosmo's production and is not on any kind of allocation.

Ames has been having a slow period, and consequently its production is running about 50 percent of capacity. This means that the company will be able to take on the Archer contract and guarantee the delivery dates. Ames certainly wouldn't have any difficulty delivering the first 100,000 feet within three months.

In the past, Ames had some quality control problems. Archer bought from this manufacturer before and, over the years, experienced an average of 3 percent rejects. The Ames salesman claims that his company just introduced a new quality control program and should therefore be able to do "a lot better." Its three tube production mills incorporate both the TIG welding operation and a mirror finish polishing operation.

One of the strong points of the organization in the past was its close contact with customers and its willingness to solve problems and provide technical assistance. However, because of its relatively poor financial situation, Ames had to lay off many of its technical service representatives, so there will necessarily be some drop in the quality of this service.

Being a division of a major steel company, Ames is naturally unionized by the Iron and Steelworkers Union. Labor relations have traditionally been excellent. This is especially true now, for both labor and management are pulling together to get the company over the rough spots.

CHOICE 2: ZENITH TUBE

Zenith Tube specializes in ornamental stainless tubing. Located in Philadelphia, the company has built its business on the slogan "Quality control means customer satisfaction." Their performance has lived up to their motto, for they will guarantee a maximum rejection rate of 0.5 percent. For any shipment that goes beyond that rate, Zenith will replace all defective tubes free of charge.

Zenith's price for the Archer contract would be $495,000. Being one of the leaders in the stainless tube industry, this company tends to charge a higher price than many of its smaller competitors. Zenith just negotiated its allocation agreement with one of the major steel producers. It will therefore be assured of a more than adequate supply to handle the Archer job.

Zenith's production schedule is sufficiently flexible to guarantee that Archer's delivery requirements will be met, and there will be no trouble delivering the first 100,000 feet of tubing within three months.

Despite the fact that Zenith is a leading stainless tube producer, it has been rather slow to introduce TIG welding mills. In fact, it could not fill Archer's initial order exclusively with TIG-welded tubing since only one of its three production mills has TIG facilities; the other two are equipped for high-frequency welding only. Zenith's production people say that they could easily ship half of the tubes with a TIG weld, and their technical service group has taken pains to point out that even if there should be trouble with the high frequency tubes, Zenith's quality guarantee would cover any losses. All three mills, however, have outstanding polishing operations, and the resulting mirror finish is absolutely top quality.

Zenith is run by a "benevolent despot" who resisted unionization until a few years ago, when he allowed an obscure local group to organize his workers. Labor relations, however, are good, because Zenith pays higher wages than any competitor. Despite this happy picture, the Iron and Steelworkers

Union is trying to make inroads into the company, so far with little success.

CHOICE 3: HAZLETON PRODUCTS

Hazleton Products is a northern New Jersey stainless tube specialist, after Zenith the largest tube producer in the industry. Its success has been due partly to careful control of inventories and intelligent purchasing of its basic steel coils. For example, last year Hazleton bought the entire stock of a failing warehouse and realized a significant saving. Consequently it has in stock more than enough steel to fulfill the Archer contract.

If this company has a flaw it is that its production capacity occasionally becomes overburdened. That is the case at this time, and the result is that Hazleton would only be able to deliver 75,000 feet of the first 100,000 feet of tubing by the time Archer is ready to start production. Hazleton points out that this situation is temporary and that the first 75,000 feet of stainless steel tubing would be more than enough to keep Archer's production going for 60 days, after which time the second installment of 25,000 feet would be ready. There should therefore be no interference with Archer's schedule.

Hazleton has TIG welding mills of sufficient capacity to fill Archer's entire order with TIG-welded tubes. Similarly, its polishing capability will meet Archer's specifications.

Because of its favorable inventory situation, Hazleton can beat Zenith's price. The total charge would be $480,000.

Hazleton's quality control is judged to be average compared to industry standards. Archer's prior experience with this manufacturer indicates that 1.5

percent to 2 percent rejects are to be expected. While Hazleton does not have a technical service group per se, its salesmen have been cooperative in the past in providing service and solving problems with quality control, and rejections have generally not been severe.

The labor situation at Hazleton is stable. Several years ago, when the Iron and Steelworkers Union organized the workers, there was some unrest, and the resulting strike shut down the plant for several weeks. Since that time, however, relations between management and labor have generally been positive.

CHOICE 4: FUTURA STEEL

This manufacturer is the smallest of the four bidding for the Archer contract. Located in Philadelphia, the company has rebounded from several lean years and has worked itself into a relatively strong and competitive position. Because it lacks inventory space, Futura Steel cannot maintain a large stock of basic steel. Its salesmen promote this factor as a benefit saying that the firm's overhead is lower than that of its bigger competitors and that it can pass the savings on to its customers. The company is bidding this job at $460,000.

Futura Steel does not have an allocation agreement with a steel producer. It advertises this, too, as a virtue, pointing out that when the firm needs steel, it shops around and buys at the best price. In order to bid on the Archer job, Futura got preliminary prices from several of the big producers.

This lack of firm allocation agreements hurt Futura during prior shortages, but management believes that there will be no problems with supplies this year. If this company gets the Archer contract, it intends to buy its steel periodically as it produces the tubes. This means that it will be able to shop around and take advantage of any price reductions that may occur later in the year.

Futura's production capacity is sufficient to meet the ninety-day delivery deadline for the first shipment. Its mills have TIG welding capability, but the polishing operation has not been up to industry standards. Management is aware of this problem and has made arrangements for a subcontractor to do the polishing.

Aside from polishing problems Futura's quality control record is outstanding—a return rate of less than 0.5 percent. This record can be attributed to the quality-control staff, which doubles as a technical services group. This group serves as a liaison between production and the customer and uses the feedback from the latter to improve the quality of the former.

Relations between management and labor have generally been good. Futura Steel has been unionized since its formation twenty years ago.

DEFINING THE ENDS

Before Archer can decide from which of the four bidders it should buy its steel tubing, it must develop rational criteria for evaluating the alternatives; it must define its ends before evaluating the available means. As we have seen in the preceding chapter, this involves the following steps:

- Establishing the need for action (*opportunity* for improvement, *dissatisfaction* with the current situation, or perceived *risk*).
- Identifying the *basic goal.*
- Defining the evaluation criteria:
    Defining the inflexible *constraints.*

35

Defining the more or less flexible *objectives*.
Defining the *priorities* of the objectives.

The Need for Action

There can be no question about the need to act in Archer's case. The company's motive for entering the buying decision process is the *opportunity* to expand its business through the Fowler contract.

The Basic Goal

In the second step, the organization must define the basic goal of the decision so that its attention will be focused on the relevant alternatives. Strictly speaking, Archer's primary goal is to fulfill the Fowler contract in the most profitable way, for that is what the company is in business for: to make a profit.

If the goal is defined in this broad manner, one of the alternatives would be for Archer to manufacture its own tubing. However, we have said that Archer decided at the outset that the high cost of the tube manufacturing equipment prohibits it from considering this option. Archer therefore narrowed down the original definition of its basic goal from "most profitable fulfillment of the Fowler contract" to "selection of the best steel tubing supplier." Without this initial decision the basic goal might well have been to choose the best supplier, not of steel tubing, but of steel.

Constraints

Once the need for action has been established and the basic goal has been defined, the next step is to develop the criteria for selecting the supplier. Here the sequence should be to decide on constraints, then on more flexible objectives, and finally on the relative importance of those objectives.

The most obvious constraint in Archer's case is the $500,000 budget. Management has decided that it cannot exceed that figure. To be considered at all, any supplier must meet that limit. In addition there is Fowler's stipulation that Archer use a guaranteed source of steel. Fowler has written that condition into the contract, therefore it clearly limits Archer's freedom to select a supplier.

In analyzing the case you may have identified other factors which might qualify as constraints. While there are not hard and fast rules about where to draw the line between constraints and objectives, it is useful to remember that the more limitations you impose on your decision, the greater the chance that you are excluding viable alternatives from consideration. For instance, if Archer decided that one of its constraints in the decision was that it must deal with a local supplier so as to save freight costs, it might have excluded a nonlocal tube manufacturer that was willing to lower its price to make up for the transportation costs. In general, therefore, it is advisable to keep constraints to the minimum.

Also, it helps to make constraints as specific as possible. In our example, both "$500,000 maximum cost" and "guaranteed source of supply" are clearly defined conditions. A tube supplier either has a guaranteed source of steel or he does not, and he charges either up to $500,000 or more.

Objectives

Next, a list of specific objectives should be compiled. In Archer's case, this list might look as follows:

Supplier in the local area.
Lowest price.
1 percent maximum rejects.
Technical service provided by supplier.

Tubing with mirror-finish polish.

Tubing welded by tungsten inert gas method.

Delivery of the first 100,000 feet of tubing in 90 days.

Unionized supplier.

When deciding on objectives it is easier simply to list them without worrying about priorities. Once you have identified everything you want to achieve, then it is time to worry about which objectives are more important than others. In compiling your list, it may often be advisable to mention as objective an item that has already been established as a constraint. In the case of Archer's budget, for example, management decided that it cannot spend more than $500,000. That is a constraint. In addition, Archer naturally wants to spend as little as possible. That is an objective. If Archer were selecting a supplier purely on the basis of price, therefore, any supplier charging more than $500,000 would not be considered, and of those who could meet Archer's budget constraint, the one with the lowest price would be the best.

Priorities

Setting priorities is again a matter of diligent judgment; there are no simple rules for it. Let us assume that Archer decides on the following priority ranking of its objectives:

1. First shipment of 100,000 feet of tubing in 90 days.
2. Lowest price.
3. 1 percent maximum rejects.
4. Mirror-finish polish.
5. TIG-welded tubing.
6. Technical service provided by supplier.
7. Supplier in the local area.
8. Unionized supplier.

Archer now has a complete set of criteria for evaluating suppliers. It has, in effect, designed an image of the ideal supplier, who meets not only the constraints but also all the objectives perfectly. Life being what it is, none of the bidders will come up to that ideal, but the one most closely matching it will clearly be the best choice.

EVALUATING THE MEANS

There are four suppliers bidding for the business: Ames, Zenith, Hazleton, and Futura. Archer's task is to pick the one that best meets its criteria as established in the first phase of the decision process. As we saw in our chapter on "systematic buying," the evaluation phase consists of four steps, each of which can be viewed as the answering of a question:

Do any alternatives not meet my constraints?

Do any alternatives carry unacceptable risks?

How well does each alternative meet each of my objectives?

Which of the alternatives meets most of my relatively important objectives best?

Archer must answer these questions for itself, in the sequence in which they are listed.

Constraints

Constraints, as we have said, are inflexible. Any supplier not meeting one or more of them cannot be considered further. In Archer's case, there were two constraints: the $500,000 budget limit and the condition of guaranteed steel supply, the latter constraint having been imposed by Fowler.

All four suppliers meet Archer's budget constraint. Ames bid was $450,000, Zenith $495,000, Hazleton $480,000, and Futura Steel $460,000. Note that the only concern at this point is that the offers be *within* the $500,000 limit; differences in price will be dealt with later.

Moving on to the condition of guaranteed steel supply, however, one company, Futura Steel, does not measure up in this respect. The others have either contracts or sufficient inventories. Futura has neither, hence there is no sense considering this manufacturer further. After examining the alternatives as to their compatibility with the constraints, Archer can then focus its attention on three companies.

Unacceptable Inherent Risks

At this point Archer must ask itself whether there are *unacceptable risks* attached to any of the remaining choices. As with violations of constraints, a positive answer would eliminate the alternative in question.

Neither Zenith nor Hazleton seems to pose unacceptable risks. Perhaps there is a remote possibility that dealing with Zenith, which is resisting unionization by the Iron and Steelworkers, will lead to labor problems for Archer. However, the risk is probably acceptable because Zenith is not altogether non-unionized and its relations with labor are good. In Ames's case, however, there is a distinct possibility that the parent company, Cosmo Steel, will close it down within the next year. If that should happen, Archer's supply of tubes would be cut, and Archer, in turn, could not meet Fowler's tight production schedule. Dealing with Ames, therefore, carries a risk that Archer should not run, and hence that supplier should be dropped from further consideration.

As with constraints, the consideration of unacceptable risks serves to narrow the buyer's focus by eliminating those choices which cannot pass critical tests. In Archer's case, Futura Steel was dropped because it violated a constraint, and Ames because it carried with it a risk that was unacceptable to Archer. The decision thus is narrowed to Zenith or Hazleton. Archer's task now becomes to examine how well each one meets the objectives Archer has set.

Objectives

Archer must now examine each objective and compare how close each of the two remaining alternatives comes to meeting them. Since the objectives will be considered one by one, Archer should follow its priority list, looking at the most important objective first and at others in descending order of priority.

Archer's top-priority objective was to have the first shipment of 100,000 feet of tubing within 90 days. Of the two choices, Zenith can deliver all 100,000 feet within 90 days, but Hazleton can only guarantee 75,000 feet. Zenith therefore performs better with respect to the most important objective. If Archer had no other objectives, the decision could be made at this point, and Zenith clearly would be the winner.

There are other objectives, however, and with the second, namely "lowest price," the situation is reversed, for Hazleton's $480,000 price beats Zenith's $495,000. This illustrates the importance of priorities in buying, for if the decision were made now, on the basis of these two objectives, Zenith would still be the better choice because it performs better on the top-rated objective while Hazleton has an edge with respect to a lesser objective. On the other hand, if the priorities were reversed—if Archer were more interested in lowest cost than in delivery of the first shipment of 100,000 feet of tubing within 90 days— Hazleton would be the better final choice.

In Archer's case, there were six additional objectives playing a role in the decision. Table 1 shows

Table 1. Comparative performance of the two finalists.

Rank	Objective	Hazleton	Zenith
1	First 100,000 feet within 90 days	75,000 feet	*100,000 feet
2	Lowest price	*$480,000	$495,000
3	1% maximum rejects	1.5%–2%	*0.5% guaranteed
4	Mirror-finish polish	yes	*top quality
5	TIG-welded tubing	*100% TIG	50% TIG
6	Technical service	through sales staff	*yes
7	Philadelphia location	Northern New Jersey	*Philadelphia
8	Unionized company	*major union	local group

Hazleton's and Zenith's comparative performance with respect to all eight objectives. An asterisk prefixed to an entry under *Hazleton* or *Zenith* indicates superior performance with respect to the relevant objective.

Putting the Priorities to Work

As Table 1 makes clear, Zenith is the final winner. It beats Hazleton on objective 1, canceling Hazleton's better performance on the next objective, price; it does better on ranks 3 and 4, more than canceling Hazleton's superiority on rank 5; and it outperforms Hazleton on objectives 6 and 7, comfortably making up for Hazleton's superior performance on the lowest-priority objective, unionization.

The Archer case is a good demonstration of the compromise nature of decisions. Different alternatives typically perform well in different areas. Without careful setting of priorities, Archer would be constantly weighing the relative merits and flaws of the two finalists, Zenith and Hazleton, without any means of deciding which is better. Having established an order of importance for its various objectives, Archer avoids that confusion. Two different people might set the priorities differently—one might rate price highest, the other delivery. The result would be that one person would choose Hazleton and the other Zenith. But both would probably be satisfied with their choice because they achieved what was most important to them and compromised in areas of lower priority.

CONCLUSION

The lesson we should learn from this is that the competitive edge between two similar products is not inherent in the products but rather in the objectives and priorities of the buyer. The outcome of the buying decision depends on the buyer's requirements and aims and on the relative importance he attaches to each of them. Any salesman trying to gain an edge on his competitors, therefore, had better look to his prospect's objectives and priorities. In our example, the salesman from Zenith would want to ensure that the objective of receiving the first 100,000 feet of tubing within 90 days was rated highest. The Hazleton man, on the other hand, would want to see the lowest-price objective at the head of Archer's priority. The salesman who can get the prospect's priorities ordered in a way that singles out his product will make the sale. In other words, the competitive edge exists in the buyer's perceptions, not in the salesman's product. The salesman, therefore, must work with those perceptions, developing them in a way that will point the buyer toward his product or service. Simply talking about a product will not get the job done—a STEAM HEAT sign will sell a room only to someone who has placed steam heat at the top of his list of objectives.

Fortunately for salesmen, very few people make buying decisions systematically. There is therefore ample opportunity for the salesman to work with a prospect to help him develop his evaluation criteria, sharpen his constraints, objectives, and priorities. It is in this development process that the sale is made. Buying is decision making. Selling is developing decisions.

THREE

ENGINEERING THE BUYING DECISION

In an article now considered a classic, Theodore Levitt analyzed a phenomenon he called marketing myopia. The myopia in question was the persistent inability or unwillingness of companies to see past their products to the customers who were actually using them. These companies failed to understand that their products did not exist in a vacuum, that no matter how brightly they shined and no matter how well they were produced, they were only as good as their ability to meet customer requirements. These companies, in other words, lost sight of the fact that a product is nothing but a means by which a buyer achieves certain ends. The value of the product exists solely in its ability to meet those ends. The *competitive superiority* of the product exists in its ability to meet those ends better than the other choices available to the buyer. Value, like beauty, is in the eye of the beholder, not in the product.

An excellent example cited by Levitt is the situation of the railroads. Somehow, railroad management slipped into the belief that railroads were an indispensable institution, a product with intrinsic value independent of its customers. They thought that their customer's basic goal was to select a railroad, whether for travel or shipping. In fact, the customers were interested in *transportation*. Their primary goal, in other words, was to choose the optimal means of transportation, and railroads were but one alternative. Furthermore, given their basic goal, there were a number of objectives relating to speed, efficiency, comfort, and cost that made the railroads a poor choice compared with their competitors in the transportation business.

The railroads, then, were guilty of being product- instead of customer-oriented; or to put it differently, they forgot that selling is engineering (no pun intended) the customer's buying decision. You cannot engineer a decision unless you focus on the prospect's basic requirements and criteria. Had the railroad companies stopped to think that they were in the business of satisfying customer transportation objectives, they might have expanded their operations to include other, more attractive, forms of transportation, thereby getting their product line to match the demand. Instead, they focused their attention on their product, thereby missing the signals the customers were sending.

Many companies, of course, conduct continuous market research programs to avoid just this sort of situation. Market research, after all, is aimed at identifying and analyzing buyer criteria. You cannot be sure exactly what buyers want unless you ask them the right questions and listen carefully to what they have to say. That is the function of market research.

Companies that keep their focus on their customers are likely to have a responsive, evolving line of products and services that sell. They are ready to adjust to changes in buyer criteria. Companies focusing only on their products, by contrast, tend to have static product lines. They do not recognize the pressures to change, to make the improvements necessary to match the public's continuously evolving criteria. A static product line in the face of changing customer criteria is a sure formula for eventual extinction.

Systematic selling is not unlike market research. Like the market researcher, the systematic salesman must identify and analyze buyer criteria before he can present his product. The difference, of course, is that whereas market research concerns itself with statistical averages, the salesman must deal with individual customers. Recall, for instance, the buyer for the chemical company who wanted to deal with a salesman "who knows us down to our underwear." Such thorough customer knowledge would not be required to do effective market research, but it is indispensable for selling.

Many salesmen, unfortunately, make the kind of mistake that the railroads made. They never stop to think about the customer's requirements. At its best, selling is market research on an individual scale; at its worst, it is simply describing your product and passing out the latest brochures.

The salesman concentrating on his customer is able to engineer buying decisions. The salesman who is merely a product spokesman cannot hope to do so because he concerns himself only peripherally with the decision maker. As we have seen, the buying decision is foreordained once the buyer's criteria are set. If you do not make these criteria your own concern from the very start, you have no chance to develop the buyer's decision. You may be supplying data that the customer can use as he evaluates the various alternatives, but you certainly do not exert any influence on the decision process. In short, you are not selling.

All that is very well. It is easy to say that salesmen, like companies, should be customer- rather than product-oriented. The problem has always been: how?

It is here that our model of the systematic buying decision becomes useful. That model gives us a tool for understanding the steps by which the customer should arrive at a buying decision and enables us to respond appropriately. We have said that systematic buying involves two successive phases: defining the ends and evaluating the means. Systematic selling must preserve the order of these basic elements; it must mirror the sequence of the systematic buying decision. It would hardly be productive, for instance, to make your presentation before you and the prospect clearly understood and agreed upon the prospect's evaluation criteria. The most desirable sequence in a sale, then, is first to identify the buyer's criteria, and second to present the product as a logical response.

The first phase, which corresponds to the buyer's task of defining his ends, requires that you gather all the relevant information from the customer: his motive for taking action, his basic goal, and his constraints, objectives, and priorities. In phase two, you must provide the customer with that information about your product which answers his concerns and enables him to evaluate the product. Both steps, then, involve communication: In the first, your task is to elicit information and be open to any signal from the prospect; in the second, you must convey information to the customer in the most effective way.

To come up with an appropriate response to the

information gathered in phase one obviously requires some thinking on your part. You must analyze the information you obtained, separate important items from irrelevant ones, determine how the buyer's criteria relate to various qualities of your product, and formulate your plan for an effective presentation. In other words, a more complete view of the sales process would contain an intermediate "analysis" phase.

Finally, you must keep up a continuous flow of information after the sale to ensure that your product *remains* a logical response to the customer's criteria; if the criteria change, you may have to see to it that the product or product package is adjusted accordingly. In other words, you must provide continuous sales service that is responsive to the customer's needs.

In summary, the sales process consists of four basic steps:

1. Identifying the buyer's criteria.
2. Analyzing how these criteria relate to your product and developing your sales strategy.
3. Presenting your product as a logical response to the buyer's criteria.
4. Servicing the account, making sure that your product remains a logical response to the buyer's needs.

In the remainder of this chapter, we will briefly discuss these four basic steps.

IDENTIFYING THE BUYER'S CRITERIA

The first interview in a multiple-interview sale (or the initial period of the first interview in a single-interview sale) is reserved for the task of identifying the prospect's needs and evaluation criteria. While this need not be a passive gathering of information, keep in mind that excessive attempts at reshaping of criteria in this early phase may hurt your credibility as a customer-oriented salesman. The buyer will feel, probably correctly, that you are more interested in making a sale than in solving his problems.

In eliciting the information you need, our model of the buying decision process provides a useful blueprint for structuring the conversation. In particular, it helps you proceed in the right sequence. As we saw in the preceding chapters, there are five successive steps involved in defining the buyer's ends:

Establishing the *motive* for entering the decision process.
Defining the *basic goal* of the decision.
Identifying inflexible *constraints*.
Defining all more or less flexible *objectives*.
Deciding on the *priorities* of these objectives.

This is the order that is most likely to lead to a satisfactory decision, and since you are vitally interested in customer satisfaction, it is the order that you should adopt in your questioning. Probe for the buyer's motive first, then for his basic goal, and finally for his detailed criteria—his constraints, objectives, and priorities. If you notice that the prospect's answers begin to stray away from this basic sequence, gently try to lead him back to it. It will make both his and your task easier.

The Opening Statement: Getting the Motive

Your very first objective is to get the prospect to evaluate his situation and agree that it could be improved (whether or not it is satisfactory) or that there are serious risks that call for action on his part. In other words, you must establish, for both him and yourself, that the customer has a valid motive to enter the decision process, namely an attractive opportunity for improvement of his situation, justified dissatisfaction with his current circumstances, or a perceived risk that the situation might deteriorate.

If you cannot get the prospect to agree that there is a genuine need for him to act, there is no sense in your proceeding any further; you would only be wasting sales time that could be spent more profitably with prospects that do have a reason to consider your product. It is important, therefore, to make absolutely certain that both you and the prospect understand that there is a motive for action and that you agree on its exact nature. The simplest and most effective way of checking on this is to use control questions and a summary:

> "Let me make sure I understand what you've just told me. You said that for the last six months you've been particularly concerned about . . . . We also talked about the possibility of a shortage of . . . supplies, and we both agreed that there's indeed a good chance of that happening. Is that correct, or did I miss anything important?"

Your main problem at this initial stage, of course, is to ask the kinds of questions that will induce the customer to talk about his goals and troubles. There are two obvious sources of information that you can draw upon for this: your knowledge of your product and your knowledge about the customer's situation. You would be a very poor salesman if you weren't informed about the product you're selling, and knowing the typical needs and problems that it addresses, you have an excellent starting point for developing an accurate profile of your customer. In a way, you are starting with an image of the "ideal" prospect, one who has all the objectives that your project is designed to meet, and your task is to determine in what respects the individual customers differ from that ideal.

If you are selling vacuum cleaners, for instance, you will be well aware of the problems typically confronting a person trying to clean a home or office; similarly, if you are selling small airplanes, you know what are the questions worrying executives with heavy travel requirements. Furthermore, the more you know about the problems that a particular company faces, the easier it will be for you to unearth a reasonable motive for considering your product.

The subject matter of your questions, then, will generally be dictated by the product you are representing, in particular, by the needs it was designed to fill. Your goal is to establish the fact that the prospect has a valid motive, based on his own basic needs, to consider your product.

Questioning for the Buyer's Basic Goal

Having established that the prospect does indeed have a valid motive for entering the buying decision process, you must work with him to identify his area of major concern. Very frequently, the buyer may have a distorted view of what his basic goal is, and you may be able to correct him at this early stage. For instance, the person who is worried about getting up his driveway under snowy conditions may have defined his goal too narrowly as that of selecting the best four-wheel-drive vehicle, and the salesman representing a snow removal service would want to point out to him that his true goal calls for consideration of a wide range of products and services that he has neglected because of his faulty definition.

The basic question for this step, then, is: "What is your area of primary concern?" The answer to this question will, to a large degree, determine the nature of the prospect's constraints, objectives, and priorities, all of which derive naturally and logically from the basic goal. As with the buyer's motive for entering the decision process, it is crucial that you ascertain his agreement with your view of his problem. This again calls for the use of control questions and a summary statement:

"If I've understood you correctly, your main concern is to make sure that you can get up that driveway of yours in the winter when there are two or more inches of snow. You were thinking of four-wheel-drive vehicles, but we agreed that there may be a good many other alternatives that would serve your purpose just as well and that it would be worth your while to explore those possibilities. Is that correct?"

Identifying the Buyer's Constraints

The most common constraints limiting the prospect's choice relate to four resources: money, time, space, and work force. Any product, including the one you're selling, uses some of these, and you have to find out exactly where the buyer's limits are. Without that information, you may be trying to sell him the wrong product, or you may genuinely be wasting your time on somebody who isn't a prospect for any of your products.

Again, it is not rare that buyers impose artificial constraints on their decisions, and this may call for correction at this early stage. For instance, the prospect may tell you that any car he considers must cost less than $4,500. It is unlikely that this is a true constraint, for there is the possibility of financing the car. While it is usually best to leave the discussion of price until later in the sales process, it may occasionally be advisable to point out, during the information-gathering phase, that the customer has adopted one or more constraints that narrow his focus inappropriately, thereby excluding viable alternatives.

Identifying the Buyer's Objectives

Your next task is to question the prospect for specific objectives. You're guided in this by two pieces of knowledge: of the product or service that you are selling and of the prospect's motive for entering the buying decision process. To know your product obviously means to know what kind of general objectives it was designed to meet, and those are the ones you will be probing for. Being informed about the buyer's motive to take action means that you have details about his reasons for dissatisfaction with an earlier buying decision, about specific risks that he is worried about, or about an opportunity that interests him.

As with the prospect's basic goal and his constraints, it may be possible to do a certain amount of reshaping. In the case of objectives, this takes two forms: changing a specific objective and adding new objectives. Often this can be done simply by slight rephrasing of a stated objective. To be effective, this calls for getting the prospect's explicit agreement to the restated version of the objective in question.

Generally, the presentation provides better opportunities for reshaping of objectives than does the information-gathering phase. Also, it must be kept in mind that engineering the buying decision is not the same as *manipulating* it. If you attempt to redefine too many of the customer's objectives, you will lose your credibility as a customer-oriented salesman.

Getting the Buyer's Priorities

The last step in the information-gathering phase of the sales process is to identify the prospect's priorities. In most cases, buyers do not have a very elaborate hierarchy of objectives; rather, they tend to divide them into no more than two rough classes: "important" and "not so important."

This is the area with the best opportunity for the salesman to influence the decision, for he can help the customer define his priorities more exactly, and more often than not, this will work to the salesman's advantage as well.

Ranking objectives according to relative importance is an intricate task that is best left to the presentation stage. In the initial interview, the salesman's job is merely to determine how the prospect views his objectives—which ones he regards as crucial and which ones seem of lesser importance to him.

Developing Your Sales Strategy

If you did your job in the fact-finding phase, you now have as clear an idea of the buyer's ends as the buyer himself. Your next task is to apply your understanding of the systematic buying decision to the information that you have gathered.

There are two separate problems involved in this. First, you must evaluate your product or service in the light of the buyer's criteria. This requires that you put yourself in the customer's position and mentally go through the buying decision process. There are two possible outcomes: Your product emerges as the best choice, or it doesn't. In the first case, your next problem is to prepare a presentation that demonstrates to the customer that your product is indeed his best alternative. In the second case, your problem naturally is more difficult. There are two options that you can pursue: redesign your product so that it meets the buyer's criteria, or change the buyer's criteria.

Seeing Your Product through the Customer's Eyes

As we discussed in the preceding two chapters, the evaluation phase of the buying decision comprises four basic steps, which can be viewed as a series of questions:

- Are there any alternatives that fail to meet the buyer's constraints? If yes, they cannot be considered further.
- Are there any unacceptable risks attached to any alternative? If so, it must be discarded.
- How well does each alternative meet each of the buyer's objectives?
- Which alternative meets most of the buyer's important objectives? This is the buyer's best choice.

You must answer these questions for yourself before you can develop an effective sales presentation. As a result, you may reach the conclusion that your product performs relatively poorly with respect to the buyer's evaluation criteria. As indicated earlier in this section, there are two things you can do to save the situation, and often you should do both of them to some extent: redesign your product or change the buyer's criteria.

Redesigning your Product

It is an error to think of products as inflexible objects. Price, delivery schedule, and quality standards are examples of product properties that are in principle changeable. If you feel that your product is not competitive in certain of these flexible areas, it may well be your best move to get management's collaboration in improving those weak spots before you attempt to make a presentation. This is one of the important differences, in fact, between a "product spokesman" and a true salesman.

Changing the Buyer's Criteria

As we said, buyers do not always act rationally in all respects. Often there is a genuine need to redefine their criteria, not just in order for you to make a sale, but because it is in the customer's own interest.

In reshaping the buyer's criteria, you should again follow the basic order defined by our model of the buying decision process: establish and sharpen the buyer's motive for taking action, then define, and possibly redefine, his basic goal, next examine his constraints, sorting out true from artificial ones, then take a look at his objectives, and finally work on his priority list. In addition, you must be on the lookout for risks inherent in your competitors' products; there may well be items here that the prospect has overlooked, especially if he has used a product for a long time, reordering it as a matter of habit.

The Presentation

Having done your analytical homework, you are now in a position to present your product as a logical response to the customer's needs. This involves four basic steps:

Review the buyer's criteria.
Identify and evaluate your product:
    Show that it is compatible with the buyer's constraints.
    Evaluate the risks attached to it.
    Evaluate its performance with respect to the buyer's objectives and priorities.
Discuss selected additional benefits of your product.
Close the sale.

Reviewing the buyer's criteria is all the more important if any of them have been shaped. It is crucial that you secure the customer's explicit agreement to any revision that you propose, and the presentation is the time to either get that agreement or remind the prospect that he did in fact agree with you.

The third step, the discussion of "additional benefits," should not be confused with the type of wholesale product description that product-oriented salesmen are so fond of. The idea is to mention only those minor benefits that seem relevant to the customer's particular situation. Such marginal benefits will hardly persuade the buyer to choose your product if he is not already inclined to view it as his best choice; but they may get him to say yes more readily and happily.

The "close," treated as the all-important climax of the sale by many books on selling, should be almost anticlimactic. It follows logically from the systematic steps that preceded it; no "persuasion" techniques should be required at all. You have identified the customer's requirements and shown him that your product meets them better than the other alternatives available to him; therefore, if he does have a valid motive at all for considering a purchase, he should agree with you that the logical thing for him to do is to order your product.

Of course, some buyers seem constitutionally unable to act immediately; they need time to think their decision over. There's nothing wrong with giving them that time. In fact, this may strengthen your credibility insofar as it exhibits sensitivity to the customer's needs. This does not mean that you should simply leave and forget about the sale. Naturally, you should establish a specific time for another meeting, during which you will get the final decision. If you've made your case clearly—related your product to his requirements—chances are that his decision will be favorable. In any case, an overbearing close employing psychological devices of persuasion will be unnecessary and inappropriate.

SERVICING THE ACCOUNT

The Greek philosopher Heraclitus observed that you cannot step into the same river twice. The message he was giving us with this image is that there is only one constant: change. There is no area of life to which his idea applies more than to business. A salesman's customers constantly are facing changing situations, and presumably they are continuously adapting to these changes. Consequently, their requirements are in constant flux.

Your product may be the perfect response to the customer's needs today; yet, tomorrow it may answer not even half of them.

Once you have made your sale, your goal is twofold: You want to maintain the business that you have just established, and you want to expand the account. Maintaining the business means solving and avoiding problems; expanding it means responding to new needs and opportunities created by the customer's changing situation.

A problem with an account arises when your product doesn't come up to the customer's expectations or if his criteria have changed. In either case, solving the problem involves bringing the product's performance in line with the buyer's criteria.

To expand an existing account requires that you be alert to the customer's changing needs and spot new opportunities as soon as they develop. In short, both maintaining and expanding your accounts means that you have to concentrate continuously on the customer's concerns and requirements.

Avoiding Customer Dissatisfaction

The best way to avoid unfulfilled expectations on the part of the customer is to ensure, at the time of the sale, that he knows precisely how the product will meet each of his constraints and objectives. Earlier we made the point that most buying decisions involve a compromise of some degree. It is rare that a product will fully meet every buyer objective. As long as the customer knows precisely to what extent he has to compromise his ideal, he should not be surprised when he finds that the product he chose does not measure up to his original objectives in every respect. Because his expectations are realistic, in other words, he is less likely to be disappointed.

It is here that the difference between engineering buying decisions and manipulating them becomes most evident. The salesman who promises Rolls Royce performance and delivers something substantially less should not be surprised if he runs into service problems. You can avoid that kind of problem if you approach selling as developing satisfactory buying decisions.

Solving Service Problems

Even if you have prepared the customer for the kinds of compromises that your product represents, problems sometimes do occur, not because of poor decision making but because of some flaw in the product package. The product per se may be adequate, but the individual specimens delivered may exhibit some imperfections. In such a case, the buyer will feel that his expectations, which were reasonable, have been disappointed, and it is your job to solve the problem at hand. There are two tasks confronting you: defining the problem and deciding what to do about it.

Defining the problem involves identifying the specific expectations that were not fulfilled. You need to understand clearly to what extent your product's performance did not live up to the relevant objectives. Next, you must analyze your own situation. This is not unlike examining the buying-decision process.

First, you will want to make sure that you do indeed have a *motive* for taking action; it is conceivable that the problem account is not worth worrying about. In general, however, you have a strong motive: You don't want to lose the account. After all, why did you seek the account in the first place if not because it was important to you?

Next, your *basic goal* is clear: You want to eliminate the variance between the product's actual and expected performance.

Generally, you must operate under two kinds of *constraints:* those dictated by the customer and your own company's. The customer usually has a time constraint: He wants the problem rectified as soon as possible. Your company has budget as well as time and manpower constraints: There is only a certain amount of money that can be spent on service, and there are a fixed number of service people available, who must budget their time. These resource constraints can severely limit the range of solutions that you are able to develop.

Next you should identify your specific *objectives*

with regard to the service problem at hand. Generally, they will follow directly from your goal to eliminate the problem in all its aspects. However, there may be additional related objectives that you should consider. For instance, in certain cases, getting rid of the problem proper may not be sufficient to placate the customer, and you may have to offer him additional incentives if you want to keep the account.

The area of service problems highlights the importance of engineering systematic buying decisions in the first place, of helping the customer develop complete and clear buying criteria. Without that groundwork, you create a number of unnecessary problems for yourself:

- You cannot tell whether there is a legitimate service problem based on a genuine variance between actual and expected product performance.
- You cannot specify the problem precisely since there were no precise criteria.
- Consequently, you have difficulty deciding how to solve the problem, which decreases your chances of repeat business with the dissatisfied customer.

If the original criteria on which the buyer based his choice were vague and general, subsequent dissatisfaction with the product will be difficult to define, and it will be hard to design an effective solution to the problem. If, on the other hand, you have assisted the buyer in his efforts to compile a complete list of clear and specific criteria, the task of determining whether there is a variance between actual and expected performance becomes that much easier. If there is such a variance, you know what to do about it.

If there isn't, and if, after your demonstrating this by comparing your product's performance with the stated criteria, the buyer still feels vaguely dissatisfied, this is a good indication that an important criterion remained unrecognized by both you and the customer when the original decision was made. In such a case, you will have to work together with the customer on a new buying decision. The important thing is that, having established your concern about the buyer's needs and problems, there is a good chance that you haven't lost the account.

Sales-Expansive Service

If one aspect of service is to maintain the account, the other is to expand it, to develop additional sales from it. Expanding your current accounts means continually collaborating with your customers to develop new buying decisions.

Change, as we noted earlier, is a constant principle in business. For product-oriented salesmen and businesses, this is a source of problems and perhaps ultimate failure. By contrast, customer-oriented companies and salesmen see in it a source of continuous opportunities. Each change in the buyer's situation alters his requirements, if only slightly. It could mean that the old, heretofore satisfactory way of doing things is no longer completely acceptable, that yesterday's products are in some respects becoming obsolete, or, to put it in our terminology, that the customer has a reason to be *dissatisfied* with his current situation. Similarly, a change could imply that the customer is facing new *risks* calling for new products or services. Finally, certain developments may present the buyer with new *opportunities* to improve his situation.

Unless you are alert to such changes, you will be unable to spot the motives for action that are inherent in them. Responsive servicing of your sales accounts means maintaining the continuous communication that will let you see new opportunities as they arise. If this is how you approach sales service, you will develop a relationship with the customer in which a continuing series of good buying decisions results in mutual benefits.

FOUR

THE INITIAL INTERVIEW

A product or service, as we have seen, is a means to an end. It enables the buyer to accomplish certain goals that are important to him. No one is interested in an insurance policy per se; it is bought because it represents the means to achieve the ends of protection and, possibly, of investment that the buyer has identified as important to him. A good buying decision is one in which the buyer selects the best means available. And clearly, before he can make a good choice, he must first consider in detail the ends he wants to achieve. The ends are the measure against which he can compare the products. The more detailed his identification of his ends, the more accurate and valuable his measuring device.

Systematic buying, in short, involves two basic steps: (1) defining the ends, and (2) evaluating the means.

As a salesman, you are concerned with developing quality buying decisions. Selling is a matter of matching the means—the products that you are offering—to

the buyer's ends. Like the buyer, you must preserve the natural sequence of the steps in the decision process. You must identify the buyer's criteria before you can demonstrate to him the logic of selecting your product, as the means that best achieves his ends. The two basic steps in systematic selling, then, are to gather all relevant information about the buyer's criteria and to respond to that information in a precisely aimed presentation. These two fundamental steps can be further broken down into four stages, as we saw in the preceding chapter:

1. Gather information about the ends to be matched (*initial interview*).
2. Analyze the information and develop an appropriate sales strategy.
3. Present your product as the logical response to the buyer's needs (*second interview*).
4. Provide ongoing service, keeping alert to new information and continuously adjusting your sales strategy and presentations to meet the customer's changing needs.

Note that our discussion of the sales process seems to advocate a two-interview approach to selling. However, some sales obviously can be closed during the initial interview. Two comments are in order here.

First, whether a sale requires one or two—or more—interviews with the buyer, the sequence is the same: gather information, analyze it, and respond with an appropriate presentation. That sequence should be observed in single-interview sales as well as in more complex situations calling for a number of interviews. A single-interview sale usually means that the buyer's situation was fairly simple, making it easy for the salesman to get the information he needed, develop his strategy, and demonstrate how his product

achieves the buyer's ends—all in one interview. But the simplicity or complexity of the sales situation does not change the basic sequence of steps. Both the buyer and the salesman are interested in the quality of the buying decision, and therefore, both need to analyze the ends before they can evaluate the means.

Second, even in simple sales situations, the salesman is interested in repeat business. By virtue of that fact, he must be concerned about the ongoing decisions that his customer faces. Therefore, even when a particular sale can be developed in a single interview, the salesman should still regard himself as involved in a multiple-interview relationship with the buyer.

For these reasons, our focus will be on the two-interview sales situation. The principles and procedures to be discussed, however, are directly applicable to simple single-interview situations as well. In either case, you are working with the buyer to develop a satisfactory buying decision. That means you have to work with him to define his ends before you can evaluate the means.

A FEW WORDS ABOUT PROSPECTING

Since this book is concerned with buying decisions and the ways in which the salesman can develop them, it necessarily focuses on the interaction between buyer and salesman, specifically on the sales interviews and the intervening analysis phase. It is, however, a basic fact of life in sales that before you can develop a buying decision, you must have a prospect. Just how the salesman gets his prospects depends very much on the kinds of products he sells and the industry and markets he works in. An insurance salesman's prospecting methods, for instance, are different from a chemicals salesman's. It is possible, however, to make some general points about prospecting that relate to our discussion of the buying decision process and its application in sales.

How to Define a Prospect

First, what is a prospect? To use our terminology, a prospect is a person or organization with a valid *motive* for entering the buying decision process and a *basic goal* that is compatible with the nature of your product or service. No matter how motivated to consider a purchase, a buyer whose basic goal points him away from your product area is clearly not a prospect for you.

Note that the buyer may be utterly unaware of any need to take action. Similarly, he may not have carefully defined his basic goal. Often it is your job to sharpen the buyer's awareness of a motive for making a decision and to help him define what exactly he is trying to achieve. A person or organization is a genuine prospect, then, if the *salesman* can identify a potential motive and an appropriate basic goal.

Clearly, it is better for the salesman if the buyer is aware of certain opportunities, risks, or reasons for dissatisfaction. And it obviously makes the salesman's work easier if the buyer has given some thought to his basic needs. But neither is absolutely necessary. A prospect may be unaware of his motive or basic goal. If *you* can identify the motive and the basic goal, then the prospect is legitimate.

Obviously, the stronger the buyer's motive, and the more compatible his basic goal with your product area, the better a prospect he is for you. Knowing this helps you decide on which prospects to concentrate your attention. All other things being equal, it clearly is best to spend time with a prospect whose motive and basic goal strongly point him toward your product area.

Where to Find Prospects

Excluding that most welcome but all too rare phenomenon—the prospect who calls on you—there are three sources of prospects: previous customers, referrals, and cold calls. Let us take a short look at each of these categories.

Previous customers. These often are the best prospects for new business. Two very important factors, however, determine just how good a prospect a particular customer is. The first is the quality of the previous buying decision that he has experienced with you. To put it differently, dissatisfied customers are not very good prospects for continuing business. And as we have said earlier, the way to create buyer satisfaction is to develop systematic, rational buying decisions. The buyer must understand precisely how the product he selects meets his particular criteria—how the means match his ends. If compromises had to be made in some areas, he must know why and to what degree. If the purchase implied certain risks, he should be informed about them and understand their nature so that he will experience no unpleasant surprises. Finally, the decision must have been implemented smoothly; delivery schedules and specified quality standards must have been met. In short, the previous buying decisions that you and the customer developed together must have been *quality* buying decisions for the customer to be satisfied.

The second key factor determining how good a prospect an old customer is relates to our earlier definition of a prospect as someone who has a decision motive and a basic goal that is compatible with your product area. A given customer, while perfectly satisfied with his previous buying decision, may feel that his requirements are met, at least temporarily. In that case, he is lacking a motive for considering a new purchase. Similarly, his resources may be temporarily exhausted—say, he has overspent his budget—and he must therefore be content with the status quo. Perhaps his attention has turned to areas that are not well served by your product. In that case, his new basic goal makes him a poor prospect for future business, even if the previous buying decision was a good one.

This point is important because salesmen tend to enjoy spending time with satisfied customers. It is comfortable to deal with people whose needs have been satisfied through your product and your efforts, and it is easy to delude yourself into thinking that you are developing new sales with that customer, whereas in fact he may not even be a legitimate prospect.

Selling is developing buying decisions. If you are spending time with customers who are not in a position to be involved in the buying decision process, you aren't doing your job. You aren't selling; you're just having a good time.

Of course, this doesn't mean you shouldn't *service* your accounts. Obviously, you have to make sure that there are no problems with the implementation of the last buying decision. That is an essential part of the task of ensuring continued customer satisfaction. But you have to remember that servicing is not selling. It is a separate function—necessary, but not to be confused with sales.

We have seen, then, that old customers often are the best prospects for additional business, but only if the salesman sees a potential for a new buying decision and begins to move the customer through the decision-making process toward the next sale.

Understanding these points is especially important in industrial selling. Here salesmen have a number of accounts, and typically they spend the vast majority of their time visiting them. In most cases, the sales call boils down to a service visit: "Any problems? Everything going OK? How's business? How's the golf game?"

This may be servicing, but it is not selling, because the visit is not concerned with a buying decision. There are two possible dangers: One, the salesman may be overlooking a valuable prospect; two, he may be wasting his time with a customer who is not a real prospect for new business in the near future.

In summary, customers to whom you've sold previously are good prospects provided (1) the previous buying decision was satisfactory, and (2) you can identify the possibility of a new purchase and can immediately begin to work on the buying decision. If the need for a decision can be identified but action on it must be deferred, the customer at least becomes a good future prospect for you.

Referrals. While you haven't done business with these prospects, you will have been briefed on their backgrounds by a customer or friend. Here again, the degree to which the buyer is motivated to take action and the nature of his basic goal determine how good a prospect the referral is. The salesman's job, consequently, is to learn as much as possible about these facts from his source.

This information will help him in the initial stages of contact with the prospect. Obviously, the more he knows about a prospect before he approaches him, the easier it is to plan and prepare for the initial interview. Just compare the following two openings and decide for yourself which is more effective.

"Good afternoon, Mr. Schwartz. My name is Harry Jones. I represent Goldstar Office Equipments. I was talking to your friend Mr. Ferguson yesterday, and he mentioned your name as someone who might be interested in our products."

"Good afternoon, Mr. Schwartz. My name is Harry Jones. I represent Goldstar Office Equipments. A friend of yours, Mr. Ferguson, mentioned that in your company you have been having a lot of problems with . . . If I understand correctly, in the past you have tried to take care of this by . . . , but you weren't absolutely satisfied with the results. I'd like to learn a little more about this because I believe I might be able to help you solve those problems."

In the first case, the customer will conclude that you're trying to make a sale. In the second, he will have the feeling that you care about his needs and problems, because you evidently have taken the time and trouble to find out about them.

Cold calls. This is your last source of prospects— and the toughest. With cold calls, the initiative is entirely up to you. There's only one way for you to determine who is a likely buyer: by consulting your knowledge of the product or service that you're selling. Remember what we said earlier: A product is nothing but a means by which the buyer achieves his basic goal. That basic goal is what defines the range of a product. A chain saw is a means to cut wood; anybody whose basic goal implies a possible need to cut wood is a prospect for a chain saw. For instance, the person might want to clear his property, get firewood, or drop a dead tree. Not all implications may be obvious, but everything invariably comes back to a consideration of the basic goal.

An additional source of cold-call prospects can be developed from a closer examination of the circumstances that might motivate a buyer to take action. To take an example from the life insurance industry, a good way to identify prospects is to concentrate on "changed conditions" that may occur in a person's business or private life, for instance, marriage, births, deaths, mergers and acquisitions, formations of partnerships or corporations. Each such change can be linked to a motive for entering the decision process—in this case, for considering the purchase of insurance.

The birth of a child, for instance, means new responsibilities; it intensifies or adds to the financial risks that the new father is facing. These risks provide a motive for considering some appropriate action that will eliminate or reduce them. In this example, the basic goal satisfied by insurance, namely financial protection against unforeseen losses or obligations, defines the market of prospects in a general way, and the information about "changed conditions" further refines this list by identifying individual motives for considering the product, life insurance.

Clearly then, the definition of a prospect— someone with a valid motive for entering the decision process and a basic goal that can be satisfied by your product—is the same for cold-call prospects as for referrals or prospects selected from your list of previous customers. Using these two aspects of the definition is the best way to approach specific prospects. To stay with the insurance example, the agent's basic method is to scan all local news sources to identify "changed conditions" affecting people in the community. By doing so, he learns who the individual is and why he ought to be a prospect. He is a prospect insofar as he has a valid motive, as indicated by a changed condition.

Even though prospecting, as we said, is a separate

function from selling, we have seen that it is useful to understand that buying is decision making. A prospect is simply someone on the verge of entering the decision process. Consideration of the two initial steps of the process—establishing the need for action and defining the basic goal—gives the salesman the criteria by which he can tell who is a prospect and who isn't.

THE OPENING: ESTABLISHING THE MOTIVE

Once the salesman has identified a prospect and made an appointment, his problem becomes how to handle the initial phase of the sales process. The relationship between the buyer and seller is only just beginning, and the salesman's actions at this early stage tend to have a significant impact on the way it develops. How then should he frame his opening?

The basic objective of the opening is to start the buyer on the decision process. Since that process begins with a consideration of valid motives for taking action, it's logical to focus the opening statement on that aspect of the process. Your opening, in other words, should point up why it is in the buyer's interest to evaluate his situation, and the possible ways in which certain products could help him achieve his goals. You are trying to get an agreement from the prospect that his situation, whether or not it seems satisfactory, could be improved, or that he faces certain serious risks. You are at this point *not* attempting to motivate the buyer to place his order; you're merely trying to get him to begin the decision process.

Most salesmen think of the opening as a short period, perhaps no more than a few minutes. However, the criterion for a good opening is not its duration but rather its effectiveness. It is the first step of the sales process, not simply the beginning of a conversation or a necessary ritual to be completed as quickly as possible. You may be able to make an effective opening in a few minutes, but it is conceivable that it will take up the entire first interview.

In this initial phase, you have three specific objectives, all of which are essential to your task of moving the prospect toward action: (1) to sharpen the buyer's perception of his motives for starting the buying decision process; (2) to establish your credibility and the fact that you're truly interested in his problems and not merely in making a sale; and (3) to pave the way for a discussion of his basic goal.

With regard to the first of these objectives, it is useful to remember Bishop Berkeley's famous dictum, *esse est percipi*—"to be is to be perceived." In this philosopher's view, anything that is not perceived doesn't exist. A buyer might be facing a serious risk calling for immediate action, but as long as he doesn't perceive it or believes it to be trivial, it is and will remain nonexistent for him—until it becomes a reality and forces itself into his consciousness. Similarly, the buyer may face a great opportunity, but if he does not perceive its existence or magnitude, you will have great difficulties trying to capitalize on it until you put it in clear quantitative terms—that is, until you sharpen his perception of the opportunity motive.

There are two possibilities at the beginning of the first sales interview: You either have prior knowledge of the buyer's motives and/or his basic goal, or you don't. Each of these situations demands its own methods for the opening. Let us look at the more difficult possibility first.

Opening with Limited Customer Knowledge

In a case where you have little or no prior knowledge about the account before the first interview, you obviously cannot make use of any specific buyer-oriented information for the opening statement. You are forced to deal in generalities while trying to achieve the three objectives of the opening, namely to sharpen the prospect's perception of a valid motive for considering a purchase, to pave the way for a discussion of his basic goal, and to establish your credibility and make it clear that you're interested in his problems.

Two approaches suggest themselves in this situation: (1) using an opening statement that focuses on establishing a motive, without much reference to the product, and (2) using an opening statement that focuses on the product and at the same time sharpens the buyer's understanding of his own motive for entering the decision process.

Focusing on the motive. Your task, if you choose this approach, is to demonstrate that there are some good reasons why the buyer should start the decision process. Assume that the buyer is satisfied with the status quo and sees no reason for making a change. Your goal then becomes to demonstrate that he is wrong, that his status quo could in fact be improved or is in danger of deterioration if he doesn't take some action soon. We have seen earlier that there are only three kinds of valid motives for entering the decision process:

1. The decision maker sees an opportunity to improve an already satisfactory situation.
2. He perceives a risk that his situation will deteriorate if he takes no action.
3. He is dissatisfied with his situation.

Since, as we have assumed, you lack any detailed knowledge about the account, it would be difficult for you to introduce a dissatisfaction motive in the very beginning. You may discover later that one exists, but you could hardly base your opening on the blind assumption that the prospect is dissatisfied with specific aspects of his situation. This leaves you with two motives to work with: opportunity and risk. Your task therefore becomes to identify, if possible in quantitative terms, either a specific opportunity or a risk that is relevant to the buyer.

Quantifying an opportunity or risk is a matter of documenting its extent and likelihood. The importance of this can hardly be overestimated. No buyer is going to be aroused by trivial or remote opportunities. The same is true for risks. Therefore, in order to sharpen the buyer's perception of such a motive, you need to document the extent of any opportunity or risk and make him understand that the opportunity will indeed materialize (or that the risk will indeed be eliminated) by his taking action.

In some cases, giving the necessary documentation might take a substantial amount of time, perhaps the entire first interview. An advertising agency trying to sell a new account on a new market would naturally spend a good deal of time identifying the size of the market (opportunity) as well as the buyer's chances of return from it. In less complex sales, on the other hand, an opening of this type may take only a few minutes.

No matter whether you spend much or little time, however, your goal is to demonstrate that a motive exists for beginning the decision process and to quantify its extent so that the buyer clearly perceives that it is in his interest to investigate the situation further.

Your second objective in the opening was to establish your credibility and customer orientation. Without prior knowledge of the buyer this may not always be easy. However, the very fact that you open the relationship showing concern about the buyer's circumstances—his motives, his desires to improve or protect his situation—sets you off, in the buyer's mind, from the product-oriented salesman who is interested only in getting the order.

Focusing on the product. The second method that you can use for the opening when you have no prior knowledge about the buyer involves a description of your product. However, this should not be a standardized features/benefits type presentation but should be framed in a way that concentrates the buyer's attention on his motive for entering the decision process. Remember that your product creates new *opportunities* for the buyer, minimizes *risks* previously unavoidable, or eliminates generic *dissatisfactions* that buyers heretofore had to endure. These are the aspects of your product on which to focus.

For example, some chemicals companies that used to sell certain of their products as dry powders have switched to liquid form. This means that buyers no longer have to put up with chemical dust in their plants. Prior to the introduction of the liquid products, buyers had to endure unsatisfactory working conditions. Although they were dissatisfied, however, they had no alternative. They had to accept the situation and cope with it as best they could.

The salesman in this case, being aware of the problems the buyers used to struggle with, would naturally concentrate on the dissatisfaction motive. He would quickly get agreement that the dry powders carried problems in the past and proceed to state that the new liquids were developed partly to solve these problems:

"Until recently, the only form in which the chemicals you need for your operations were available was as dry powders. People have had a lot of problems because of the dust that inevitably went along with them. They certainly didn't make for good working conditions, for example. I suppose you've experienced the same problems." (*Dissatisfaction motive;* the salesman is likely to get the prospect's agreement on this point.)

"You're probably also aware that there may soon be serious trouble because of noncompliance with the Occupational Safety and Health Act." (*Added risk motive,* again likely to draw agreement.)

"Our company has thought about this question a good deal, and we've developed a new line of liquid products that avoid these problems. With your agreement, I'd like to spend some time with you discussing what you're doing in your mills, to see if our products meet your other requirements as well." (*Preparing the discussion of the buyer's basic goal and his evaluation criteria.*)

Note that the buyer is not making a decision at this point. He is merely agreeing to begin the decision process. Perhaps the new liquids fail to meet some criteria important to him and are therefore an unacceptable alternative. But his dissatisfaction with the current dry powders probably is sufficient motive for beginning to evaluate the new liquid products.

Many salesmen confuse this kind of product-description opening with a sales presentation. That is a great mistake. What's more, they spend too much time describing every feature of the product, leaving it to the buyer to figure out how each particular feature relates to his specific objectives. And more often than not salesmen try some sort of close when they finish the description, believing that they are at the end of the process when in fact they're just at the beginning. A product description has value only insofar as it motivates the buyer to begin the process of evaluation. It should therefore concentrate on the motive and bring it into sharp focus. A full-fledged product description at this point is not only unnecessary but also counterproductive; it introduces irrelevant information unrelated to the buyer's criteria.

In order to demonstrate the value of your product, you must show that it is an effective means by which the buyer can achieve his specific ends. If there is no match between ends and means, the product has no use for him. Therefore, describing a product's "benefits" before you know the buyer's requirements is putting the cart before the horse and generally produces negative results.

Opening When You Have Prior Knowledge about the Prospect

Many times you do have information about the customer's situation before the initial interview. As a matter of fact, it is much to your advantage to secure at least some basic knowledge about the prospect, because this gives you additional possibilities for constructing your opening.

Often you may have found out about a possible motive on the buyer's part to consider a purchase in your product area. In that case, you would open the interview by identifying that motive, followed perhaps by further questions intended to expand your understanding of it. In this way, you would immediately focus the prospect's attention on his reason for entering the buying-decision process.

For example, the salesman may have learned that a particular printer has experienced quality problems with a certain type of paper that he is currently buying. The initial interview in this case might run somewhat as follows:

SALESMAN: I understand that you're not completely satisfied with some of the paper you're now buying, especially the high-gloss type, and that a certain number of customers have expressed some dissatisfaction.

CUSTOMER: Well, yes, there have been some problems.

SALESMAN: Could you tell me a little more about this? What were your specific complaints? As you may know, our company manufactures top-quality high-gloss paper, and perhaps if you tell me what kind of problems you've been having, we could come up with a solution to them.

Such an approach not only focuses the buyer's attention on his motive for taking action, it also begins the process of information gathering, your task in the first phase of the sale. Inevitably, the analysis of the buyer's reasons for dissatisfaction leads to a description of his basic goal and from there to a discussion of his evaluation criteria—his constraints, objectives, and priorities.

You may even have learned about the buyer's basic goal before the first interview. You may know, in other words, that he is sufficiently motivated to consider ways of improving his situation and that he has a reasonably clear idea of what he wants to achieve with his purchase. Of course, it is entirely possible that the definition of his basic goal will shift somewhat in the course of the sales process, but there is at least a starting point. In that case, the content of your opening statement would naturally be a summary of the buyer's motive for taking action and a description of his basic goal as you understand it. Your statement is designed to make sure that both you and the buyer are focused on the same concern and agree on the definition of what it is the buyer wants to achieve. This approach puts you in a very favorable position, because it clearly demonstrates your customer orientation. It starts the sales process off with an immediate emphasis on what the *buyer* is trying to do.

In summary, then, the function of the opening statement is to sharpen the buyer's perception of his motive for entering the buying decision process and to begin movement toward a definition of his basic goal. It furthermore has to establish the salesman's customer orientation and credibility. The duration of the opening depends solely on how long it takes to achieve these objectives, and the choice of the method depends on the degree of the salesman's prior knowledge of the buyer's situation.

The Limits of Motivation

P. G. Wodehouse's inimitable character, Jeeves, is the ultimate manipulator. He is the *deus ex machina*, the savior who arrives at the end of the story with a solution to the complex muddle his featherbrained employer has concocted. And more often than not, Jeeves' solution is based on his vast understanding of "the psychology of the individual" and his ability to manipulate it.

Had he not been a valet, Jeeves might have become a salesman, and his success would have been assured. After a brief period of research into the psychology of Eskimos, he would have had them standing in line to buy his refrigerators. No doubt he could have sold coffee to Brazil, coal to Newcastle, and jogging shoes to octogenarians—all as a result of his profound understanding of the human psyche.

Perhaps it is unfortunate, but the rest of us do not possess Jeeves' powers. The intricacies of human behavior tend to be mysterious to us, and we are more often forced to adapt ourselves to the psychology of the individuals with whom we're dealing than we are able to manipulate it.

The point is important for several reasons. First, our terms "motive" and "motivation" may create the impression that we are addressing problems of motivational psychology. Our use of these words, however, is much more restricted. We are interested only in the buyer's motive for considering a purchase—his reasons for entering the decision process. In this sense, motivating the buyer does not mean manipulating him. It simply means starting him off on the decision process by demonstrating that there is a good reason why he should do so.

Second, no profession spends more time or money learning about behavior, psychology, motivation, and similar problems than the salesman's. That is not surprising. The essence of selling, after all, is interaction between people; it makes sense, therefore, that salesmen concern themselves with the ways people behave. Thanks to this, psychologists have long been making a good living as consultants to sales organizations. And again, it is undeniably true that a salesman's success is determined in part by his skill in dealing with people. The most carefully conceived sales strategy is next to useless in the hands of a salesman with an abrasive personality or style. The most carefully designed questioning tactic is ineffective when practiced by a salesman who doesn't know the difference between asking questions and putting a prospect through the third degree.

In short, "human skills" are important in sales. The problem is, however, that no two people seem able to agree on the best method of interacting with people. In fact, the only thing on which there is agreement is that there is no one best method and that different salesmen need to use different styles in different situations or, if they do not have this flexibility, seek out prospects for whom their personalities, style, and interpersonal skills and methods are appropriate. It is difficult, if not impossible, in other words, to change your entire style or character and learn interpersonal skills that are not direct expressions of your own personality. The best you can do is to become aware of your interpersonal style and skills and work in areas in which you feel comfortable.

The customer-oriented approach to selling provides a framework and structure for the interaction between salesman and buyer. The style which the salesman uses for dealing with his prospects is up to the individual, but the fact that he must begin by motivating the buyer to enter the decision process and then lead him through it is a constant. No matter what personal variables are involved, the buyer must always be treated as the decision maker rather than somebody to be manipulated. You may conduct the opening with the panache of a Cyrano or the restraint of a Henry James; that will depend on your individual style and your ability to adapt it to new situations and prospects. But no matter what the interpersonal aspects of your opening, you still must achieve the three objectives we have identified: motivate the prospect to enter the decision process, begin moving toward an analysis of his basic goal, and establish your credibility and customer orientation. The tone of the interaction is situationally determined; the objectives of the opening are fixed.

While we are on the elusive subject of psychology in selling, it is worth pointing out that the customer-oriented approach to sales is the one most likely to dispel the prospect's misgivings (if he has any) about receiving a salesman. Your immediate objective is to understand the buyer's point of view—his needs and problems. As far as the psychology of the individual is concerned, this is a much better position than that of the product-oriented salesman, whose every move tends to reinforce the buyer's preconception of the salesman as someone interested in selling his product rather than in solving the buyer's problems.

The product-oriented salesman's basic attitude is summed up by the statement: "Let me tell you about my product." The customer-oriented salesman's basic approach, on the other hand, is: "Tell me what *you* are trying to achieve. Perhaps I can help you do it." Clearly, the second attitude is more likely to facilitate smooth interaction between buyer and seller. The salesman is perceived as somebody helping the buyer act in his own interest.

Not having Jeeves' powers, positioning ourselves on the buyer's side is the best thing we can do. And using the buying decision process as the structure of the relationship is the proper way to do it.

FINDING THE RELEVANT FACTS

Conversations are spontaneous and relatively unstructured, and the sales interview is no exception. You obviously cannot plan ahead the entire conversation for a session. Even in response to careful questioning by the salesman, the buyer will wander off the topic at hand. He may mention problems that trouble him about his current situation, along with some objectives that he wants to achieve and things he has done in the past or other products that he has used. As often as not, he'll introduce a great mass of irrelevant information, from complaints about his golf game to a complete history of his attitude on American foreign policy. Out of this tangled body of information the salesman is expected to glean the critical pieces he needs and form an accurate picture of the buyer's requirements, his basic goals, constraints, objectives, and priorities.

Although the salesman may be able to give some direction to the conversation by asking pertinent questions about the other's situation, he has no complete control over the onrush of haphazard responses from the buyer. Buyers, even when they're very conscious of the fact that they are involved in an important decision, generally do not think and talk in terms of the steps in the decision-making process. They do not, for instance, first identify their basic goal and then proceed to list their constraints and objectives. On the other hand, this is precisely the information needed by the salesman, who is trying to develop a systematic decision. The salesman, therefore, needs two things for the fact-finding phase of the sales process: a method of questioning that will stimulate the buyer to talk about his situation and a method for analyzing the buyer's total response to identify those bits of information that are relevant to the buyer's decision.

Fact finding, in short, is a matter of stimulating a response and collecting relevant information. It requires skills in questioning and listening.

Our model of the buying decision process helps with both tasks. As far as listening is concerned, it acts like a cash register drawer: It functions as a group of compartments that you can use to categorize a mass of unorganized "bills" and "change"—the various bits of information. Knowing what an objective is and how it differs from a constraint, understanding the fundamental difference between the ends the buyer is trying to achieve and the means he may already be using, knowing the nature of priorities—all this provides the salesman with a tool for collecting and organizing the relevant information from the buyer, information that often comes in a random, disorganized sequence.

As the buyer talks, the salesman isolates bits of information and classifies them: "There's an objective, but not too important. Now there's a constraint. And another one. Then there's a key objective, absolutely top priority. Now he's mentioning an alternative he's currently using and also one he's considering for the future. And now he's rambling off on some irrelevant tangent, so forget that." As the buyer talks, the salesman takes each bit of data and places it in its proper spot in the "cash drawer." He arranges the information according to its function in the decision process.

In most cases it is possible and desirable to take notes as the buyer is talking. Few buyers resent this; in fact, many become more open once you ask if they would mind your taking notes. It emphasizes the fact that you're serious about forming an accurate picture of the buyer's needs and problems. Taking notes helps you identify quickly which data represent an objective, which a constraint, and so on.

Salesmen sometimes use tape recorders to capture a maximum of information for later analysis, and often you may find this a useful technique. No matter how you collect your information, however, understanding the elements and sequence of the decision process gives you a tool for sorting through the variety of data supplied by the buyer and for capturing whatever is relevant.

Of course, no salesman can depend on the buyer to provide the initiative in the conversation. There are such buyers—people who love to talk about their situations, where they're trying to go, the options they are considering—but they are a minority. In order to be able to use the "cash register drawer," you must therefore first stimulate the conversation. Often, this requires you to ask specific questions, both to keep the talk flowing and to learn detailed facts about the buyer's situation which he might not think to volunteer.

The basic question in any sales interview is, "What are you trying to achieve?" This is an expression of customer orientation and represents our entire approach to selling. That question, however, is more a statement of philosophy than it is a practical question that you can actually use. Generally, you need to start the fact-finding stage with specifics about the buyer's goals.

The problem then becomes to ask questions that will stimulate a meaningful conversation. There are two aspects to this: content and structure.

The content of your questions is dictated by your product; their structure, or sequence, by the systematic buying decision process. Products, as we have seen, exist not for their own sake but as means by which a buyer achieves certain goals that are important to him. Products designed without prior awareness of buyers' needs soon fade into oblivion: Just as their creators were indifferent to user requirements, so buyers are indifferent to their existence. By the same token, products that do not change with changing market needs gradually wither away.

Presumably. then, your product or service originally was designed to match a certain general class of needs and has been adapted to changes in the market. It's your job to keep aware of the range of needs filled by your product, and you must use that knowledge to lend the proper focus to your questions in the fact-finding interview.

For example, a business airplane is designed to

combine the advantages of fast transportation, ready availability, scheduling flexibility, comfort, cost-effective travel, and prestige. Those are the ends the executive jet was designed to meet. A jet salesman conducting a fact-finding interview with a potential buyer would do well to focus his questioning on these areas and try to determine to what extent these generic market requirements match the individual buyer's specific ends. The salesman, in a sense, has an ideal buyer in mind—one who wants all the things his product was designed to provide. His task in the fact-finding phase is to use this ideal as a starting point from which to develop an individual profile of the actual buyer. The ideal, in short, tells him what questions to ask. If his plane is particularly cost-effective, for instance, he'll want to ask questions about the prospect's concerns in this area. The same holds true for all the other original design specifications.

It should be obvious that the more a salesman knows about a prospective buyer before going into a fact-finding session, the more specific his questions can be. This is important for two reasons. First, such knowledge enables him to zero in on those aspects of the prospect's business that are relevant to his product. If you know approximately how many miles a year a corporation's executives travel, it is easier to probe for specific cost-effectiveness concerns. Second, by asking detailed and informed questions about the prospect's business, the salesman further demonstrates his customer orientation. The fact that he took the time and trouble to learn as much as he could about the prospect's circumstances testifies to his interest in the prospect's problems and objectives. Such research into a prospect's business situation may not always be possible, but when it is, it can be most useful in the questioning process.

Our second point was that your understanding of

the buyer's decision process provides a structure for the interview: It determines the sequence of your questions. You should concentrate first on the buyer's basic goal, then move on to his constraints, objectives, and priorities. Also, if the buyer's motive for entering the decision process is dissatisfaction with his current situation, you should start by concentrating on this theme, which will be the source of many of the buyer's more specific ends. Solving his current problem may in fact be the thing most on his mind; that is, eliminating the reason for his dissatisfaction may well be his basic goal. On the other hand, the problem may be but one aspect of a larger concern that is properly regarded as his basic goal. In either case, the discussion of the problem at the bottom of his dissatisfaction naturally leads to a conversation about his general goals, besides keeping the buyer's attention focused squarely on his motive for entering the buying decision process.

How to Close before the Presentation

In a fact-finding interview, your basic objective is to develop the buyer's list of ideal criteria, the measuring stick against which he will evaluate the alternatives available. Naturally, you're interested in selling your alternative, and so your efforts in developing the buyer's ideal criteria may include your suggesting certain ones, "implanting" certain objectives that your product meets particularly well. In this way, the buyer's ultimate "ideal" is in fact a combination of his own original criteria and the objectives that you suggested to adopt. The latter category in particular includes criteria originally not perceived by the buyer but acceptable to him once they're called to his attention.

Implanting of criteria gives you a great tactical advantage. Obviously, having a thorough understanding of the original design specifications of your product, you know which criteria it meets best. As far as the buyer is concerned, the performance of your product, its superiority as a means, is determined by its effectiveness in achieving his ends. When the buyer's specific requirements match, or come close to matching, the original design specifications of your product, it is reasonable to expect that he will look upon it as his best alternative. And yet in order to gain this decisive advantage, you need not secure any agreement from the buyer beyond his acceptance of a particular criterion that he did not originate but is willing to adopt. In this way, you affect the final decision long before your product comes up for evaluation. You begin to "close" before your presentation. Obviously, if the buyer agrees that a certain objective is top priority and if your product is the only alternative capable of achieving it, then the product is a major step closer toward being selected, even before you've begun to discuss it.

Multiple Decision Makers

Often it is necessary to do fact finding at several different levels. This is especially true in industrial or corporate sales, where a wide variety of people have information on the prospect company's problems and requirements. These same people will often have something to say about the final choice. One person may be responsible for the final decision, but a number of others may make recommendations. Your task in such a situation is to conduct fact-finding interviews with each of these people.

Clearly, it would be short-sighted to deal exclusively with the purchasing agent when a vice president of operations will in fact make the final decision.

Each person typically will have a slightly different view of the company's concerns and objectives, and each is likely to have special needs and problems that may have to be considered as well.

Your best approach, then, is to identify the decision maker and all individuals in a position to make recommendations. If possible, you should conduct fact-finding sessions with each of them. The more detailed the final profile of buyer requirements, the more effective your presentation will be. As we will see, it is generally impossible to develop a presentation that is good for every situation and buyer. To have an impact, the presentation must show how your product satisfies the specific objectives that the buyer has identified. The more complete the profile, therefore, the more complete and effective the presentation.

Identifying the Buyer's Basic Goal

The buyer's basic goal is a statement of what he is trying to achieve by taking action. All the detailed criteria—constraints, objectives, and priorities—are inherent in it; they are but specific aspects or consequences of it. To put it differently, the basic goal defines the boundaries within which all specific criteria and all feasible alternatives must fall.

Many times a buyer knows what his basic goal is with regard to a particular product area. At other times, his idea of his basic goal may not accurately reflect his true requirements, and in such cases it is in both his and the salesman's interest to correct his perception and revise his basic goal appropriately. He may, for example, have defined his goal too narrowly, thereby eliminating many alternatives that deserve serious consideration since they would achieve his genuine requirements more efficiently than the alternatives to which he has artificially constrained himself.

Finally, the buyer may not have given much thought to his basic goal in a particular product area. As we mentioned earlier, this is a classic problem in life insurance sales, since most people do not want to think about that product and its intimations of mortality. Because of their reluctance to face certain disagreeable facts of life, they have formulated no basic goals in the financial services product area of which life insurance is a part.

When you're informed about the buyer's basic goal before going into the fact-finding interview, you should deal with it in the opening statement, as we have seen. More often than not, however, you lack the relevant information, and just as often, it seems, the buyer doesn't know his goal either or is focused on the wrong one. You both need to identify it before you can go on.

One of the life insurance industry's top salesmen developed a very efficient technique of questioning for the basic goal. He concentrates on the business insurance market, that is, on selling a variety of life and health products to business, primarily small corporations. In the first step, he gives the prospect an overview of his product areas, for instance, individual retirement accounts, pension plans, deferred compensation, or key man insurance. He describes in some detail each of these categories and their relation to the buyer's business concerns. After this period of description, during which he has identified about a dozen key product areas, he asks, "Which of these areas represents your number one priority?"

His real question, of course, is which of the product areas identified relates to one of the buyer's current concerns. It probably is not his top-priority concern; if it were, he would have called in an insurance adviser long before this. The salesman is using the product list to focus the buyer's attention. The areas that he listed might theoretically all be of very little interest to the prospect, but one certainly is going to be more interesting than the others. Once the salesman has an answer to his question, he has a basic goal to work with. Perhaps, as the conversation continues, he learns that the goal he extracted from the prospect needs reshaping in order to fit the situation more accurately. But using this method at least gives the salesman a starting point.

Note that in identifying these various product areas, the salesman is not talking about specific product alternatives. Each of the product areas represents a set of general buyer concerns, and within each there exist a number of specific products with which to achieve individual buyer objectives. The list of products, in other words, simply stands for a collection of common concerns. "Deferred compensation," for instance, is shorthand for the buyer's various concerns about compensating and motivating his top-management people, and those concerns all relate to the buyer's basic goal of improving compensation for his managers. In order to achieve that basic goal and all the specific objectives derived from it, there are a number of deferred-compensation plans that the agent can design. The agent, in other words, is not engaged in a product description at this point; he is simply identifying areas of common concern among businessmen, with the aim of determining which of these are of greatest interest to the buyer. From there he can begin to identify the prospect's specific constraints, objectives, and priorities, and based on that profile of ends he can design the deferred-compensation package that best suits the buyer's total requirements.

A closer analysis of this technique shows that the lengthy description of product areas essentially provides the background for one question: "What is your major concern?" The introductory description is an elaborate preparation for this question, focusing the buyer's attention on the general problems that he is likely to share with other businessmen.

This approach is applicable to any sales situation as a means of identifying the basic goal. To summarize, it calls for no more than a brief description of the common concerns related to the salesman's product area, followed by a simple question as to which of these areas is of most interest to the buyer. In a way, it amounts to asking, "What are you basically trying to achieve?" But the technique gives focus to the question and, in so doing, greatly improves the probability of getting a meaningful response.

Such an approach, it should be added, is most useful in cases where you have no real knowledge of the buyer's situation. When you do have information about the buyer's concerns and requirements, it obviously is better to translate your knowledge into specific questions that allow you to identify his basic goal.

Questioning for Constraints

There are certain common sources of constraints, and they indicate the kind of questions to be asked in order to identify the limits within which a particular buyer must operate. We said earlier that the buyer's constraints generally are related to his limited resources, specifically, money, time, space, and workforce.

A product affects resources insofar as it reduces the

need for some of them (for instance, automated machinery replaces people) or uses particular ones. Normally, of course, it does both.

For instance, an automated machine, while reducing the need for manpower, costs money, occupies space, and requires people to maintain it. In short, every product has some impact on the buyer's resources. The salesman who knows his product understands this impact. If he's selling machinery, he knows what it will cost, how many people it will take to install and use it, how soon he can deliver it and how regular future deliveries can be, how much space it will use once installed, and so on. This knowledge tells him what kind of questions he needs to ask in order to identify the limits the buyer must observe in the buying-decision process.

There are two important points to be noted about constraints: (1) by definition, constraints are inflexible and therefore limit the range of choices available to the buyer; (2) the buyer's perception of his constraints is not necessarily correct.

The second point may need elaboration. Money is a scarce resource and therefore tends to constrain the buyer severely. A person buying a car might quite naturally perceive his limits as $5,000, and if business were done strictly on a cash basis, that limit might be accurate. However, installment plans were invented to eliminate just such cash constraints, with the four-year car loan as a further step toward avoiding the constraints imposed by shorter installment plans. Therefore, the buyer who perceives his constraint as $5,000 may in actual fact be defining his limits inaccurately. Assuming that he is willing to finance his purchase, his real constraint is the amount of monthly payments he can afford.

The point is that because constraints are inflexible and limit the range of possible alternatives, the buyer must be careful to define them in a way that reflects the true limits of his resources. It is the salesman's job to help the buyer arrive at that definition. Clearly, it is in his interest to ensure that the buyer's perception of his limits is compatible with the demands the salesman's product places on his resources. This issue will be discussed in greater detail in the chapter on the sales strategy; for now it is sufficient to observe that the salesman's task with regard to constraints frequently is to alter the buyer's perception of his own limits.

There are no hard and fast rules telling the salesman at what point in the sales process he should deal with this problem. He can hold off until the presentation or attempt to alter the buyer's perception of his constraints during the fact-finding phase. In the first instance, the salesman uses the presentation to say, in effect, "You told me you had only so much money available, but I have worked out a plan that will make that money go farther." In the second instance, he immediately responds to a stated constraint: "You really don't have to think of your budget in terms of a total cash amount since installment financing is available, which will enable you to consider possibilities that your cash budget might not allow."

For our present discussion, the point is that you often need to deal with the buyer's inaccurate perception of his constraints. In more complex sales situations it may be better to delay tackling the problem until the presentation; in simple ones it is generally possible to correct the buyer's perception right then and there.

To uncover the buyer's constraints, remember that

they depend on his perceptions of his own resource limitations. Where necessary, you can prompt the appropriate response by asking how specific resources, say, people or money, are allocated now and what the buyer's particular concerns and plans in these areas are.

Questioning for Objectives

In identifying the buyer's objectives there are two basic questions to be asked: what he is currently doing and what he would like to be doing. The first of these can be regarded as questioning the prospect about his previous buying decisions, which after all are responsible for his current situation. The second question is directed at his future plans as well as at his assessment of other alternatives that he is considering.

The direction of your questioning will again depend largely on the buyer's motive for entering the decision process. If, for example, he is *dissatisfied* with his current situation—say, he has a problem with a previously selected product—your job is to find out the precise nature of the problem, its magnitude, and all its ramifications. This involves questions about the buyer's original criteria and the degree to which the products he currently uses fail to meet them. In this case, then, you're interested in what the buyer is presently doing, particularly the problems that go along with it. What he would like to do is reasonably clear: to find a way to correct or improve his current unsatisfactory situation. When the buyer's motive is dissatisfaction, therefore, your task is to probe for the problem that is troubling him until you're able to translate it into specific objectives for the decision under consideration.

For example, a driver dissatisfied with his car because of the high cost of operating it has a good reason for considering a new purchase. His motive is dissatisfaction, and his basic goal is to select a new car. His constraints probably involve budget considerations, both for purchase and operation, and his objectives derive from his problem. Possibly, his objectives might be as follows:

25 miles per gallon.
Fewest repairs.
Lowest insurance premiums.
Long warranty.
Low dealer service charges.

His basic problem, then, namely "expensive operation," has a number of aspects, each of which must be identified by the salesman; they are the objectives to be met by the new purchase. The salesman should be as specific as possible and strive to develop a complete and accurate picture of the buyer's criteria. It is not in his or the buyer's interest to assume that the buyer's sole objective is to eliminate the reasons for his dissatisfaction.

Solving a problem of this kind involves deciding on the best course of action, and as with any decision, the more detailed and specific the criteria, the better the chances of success. The salesman's probing for the buyer's acute problem may bring to light certain heretofore unperceived objectives, thereby improving the chances of reaching a quality decision. And clearly, a quality decision is not only in the buyer's but also the salesman's best interest, assuming he has a competitive product.

Developing detailed criteria, furthermore, facilitates the salesman's task in the presentation, because the sharper they are, the easier it will be for him to demonstrate how his product meets them. For instance, it is clearly easier to show that a car gets 25 miles per gallon, has a five-year guarantee, and so on, than it is to prove that it will alleviate a *general* dissatisfaction.

When the buyer's motive for entering the decision process is a perceived *risk* to his current situation, his basic goal in all probability will be to avoid the risk or minimize its negative effects. His specific objectives derive from this basic concern in a natural way. For example, the owner of a warehouse might suddenly face a risk because of his decision to add a highly volatile product to his inventory. The new risk, of course, is the outbreak of a fire, and it probably is severe enough for him to consider taking action. He may have defined his basic goal as that of selecting a sprinkling system to minimize the fire risk. His specific objectives might include the following:

Automatic system independent of human operation.
Reliability.
Low cost.
Using chemical agents.

As with the dissatisfaction motive, once you have identified a significant risk, it will be easy to determine the prospect's specific objectives. As you discuss the buyer's perception of the risk that is worrying him, you naturally come to talk about the objectives he is trying to achieve. In this situation, you are essentially asking the buyer about his plans for the future, about the kinds of results he hopes to get. The answers will yield his specific criteria on which he will base his buying decision.

When the buyer's motive for beginning the decision process is an *opportunity,* your basic question is again, "What do you want to do?" How receptive the buyer is will depend largely on how attractive the opportunity is with which you're presenting him. If he sees a chance to improve his situation in quantum leaps, he will in all probability be more than ready to answer your questions. If, on the other hand, there's nothing spectacular about the opportunity, the buyer, although motivated to begin the decision process, may not be all that willing to volunteer information or respond to questions in great depth.

Again, we're dealing with a problem of buyers' perceptions. The better a job you did in the opening phase of the interview, the sharper the buyer's perception of the opportunity will be, and the readier he will be to provide you with the relevant information. A weak opening that doesn't bring the opportunity into sharp focus is unlikely to generate buyer involvement.

Questioning for objectives when the buyer's motive is an opportunity usually is more difficult than when dissatisfaction or a perceived risk is involved. The reason is that the opportunity motive generally is external; it has been supplied by the salesman. When a buyer is dissatisfied or aware of an intolerable risk, he is normally willing to talk about his concerns, provided he feels that you may be able to help him. By contrast, when he is neither dissatisfied nor aware of a significant risk, the prospect of changing the status quo holds little attraction for him.

In short, how great the difficulties are that you encounter in questioning for objectives depends on two factors: the magnitude of the opportunity presented to the buyer and the sharpness of his perception of that opportunity. When the opportunity is significant and its perception by the buyer sharp, you probably will have little trouble, but when the opportunity is somewhat less than stunning or the buyer has no more than a vague idea of it—perhaps because your opening was weak—you will find the buyer less receptive, and it may be hard to generate information about his objectives.

In difficult situations like these, you must be prepared to ask very specific questions about the buyer's operation in order to gather the details you need to build an accurate profile of the buyer's objectives. The source for your questions is your product. As we have seen, the original design specifications for a product or service define an ideal set of buyer objectives, namely the set of objectives that the product is designed to satisfy. The sales task can be seen as matching the actual buyer's objectives as closely as possible to this ideal set; the closer the fit, the greater the likelihood that your product will emerge as the buyer's best choice.

These original design criteria, then, represent the key areas of your product's performance and therefore are the ones in which you need to probe for the buyer's individual objectives. For example, if you're selling subcompact cars, you know that your product was originally designed to meet a number of economy objectives, and its performance is measured against those objectives. When questioning an individual buyer about his particular objectives for a car, you will have to turn to the original design specifications for clues about the kinds of questions that are likely to generate objectives reasonably in tune with the character of your product.

In our example, you obviously would be ill advised to start questioning the buyer about his requirements for comfort and roominess; your questions will instead concentrate on his economy objectives—

the kind of gas mileage he wants, the maximum maintenance figures he has in mind, or the sort of insurance premiums he is ready to pay.

You know what your product is all about and in which areas it performs best. When faced with a buyer who doesn't volunteer much information about his objectives, you can fall back on your product knowledge for specific questions in each category of performance. Each of your questions, then, asks the prospect about his wishes with regard to a specific aspect of product performance, such as gas mileage or average maintenance costs. The collected answers to a series of such questions become the buyer's profile of objectives on which he will base his buying decision.

Clearly, this technique of developing specific questions about the buyer's objectives from an understanding of your product, in particular, the ideal set of criteria it was designed to meet, can be applied in any sales situation, whether the prospect's motive for entering the buying decision process is a perceived opportunity, a risk, or dissatisfaction. When his motive is an opportunity, however, chances are greater that you must use the technique; where a risk or dissatisfaction is involved, the buyer may often be more willing to talk about his objectives.

Another important source for specific questions is research. Banks, to name one example, maintain good-sized research departments providing information about client companies. Bank representatives can use this information to prepare pertinent questions about a company's objectives before going into a fact-finding interview. During the meeting, the bank representative will be able to bring up relevant areas of the client's operation and specify the client's objectives in a way that prepares him for a subsequent presentation of how the bank's services can help him meet those objectives.

The value of such research as a source for specific questions, which will generate correspondingly specific buyer objectives, can hardly be overestimated. This kind of preparation can also give you valuable indications about what the client's objectives *ought* to be. As we have seen, there often is a great discrepancy between the objectives the buyer recognizes and communicates to the salesman and those which he should have but fails to see. These unperceived objectives are inherent in his situation, and having analyzed the latter before the interview, you are able to identify them easily.

For example, corporations with large numbers of divisions frequently have a receivables problem because customers send their remittances to the individual divisions, which in turn send the money to headquarters. The effect is that headquarters loses the use of this money during the extended transition from buyer to division to headquarters. Conceivably, it might not have occurred to the company's financial manager that one of his cash management objectives is to reduce this receivables "float," especially if the situation, having been this way for some time, has become accepted as a fact of life. His unperceived objective, then, would be to minimize this float, and an additional, related one would be to reduce the personnel costs that are currently perceived as necessary to handle the inefficient receivables system.

A bank representative selling cash management services will recognize, based on his knowledge of the kinds of objectives that his services were designed to meet, that the client company should have these objectives. They are inherent in the operating conditions of the buyer and identified by the salesman, thanks to his understanding of the ends his product meets.

Generally, the best time for bringing unperceived objectives to the attention of the buyer is during the presentation, and therefore we will deal with the problem in more detail in the last chapter. For now we're interested in two points:

- Buyers do not always know what their full range of objectives should be, and salesmen, therefore, must be alert to the operating conditions of the buyer in order to spot unperceived but potentially important objectives.
- The salesman's product provides the base from which these unperceived objectives can be identified; that is, the ends that the product is designed to meet often are ones the buyer ought to have but for various reasons doesn't see.

Another important source of information about the buyer's objectives is his opinion of the alternatives that he is considering along with your product. It is often not possible to get the buyer to talk about them, but when he can discuss competitors without prejudice to anyone's cause, his perception of their performance is a good indication of the criteria he will use to make his decision. If, for instance, he is impressed with a particular aspect of a competing product's performance and dissatisfied with another, he is indicating, in effect, that his objectives are to duplicate the performance in the first area and get better performance in the other. In this way, you have learned about two important objectives that might not have emerged if you hadn't asked the buyer about the other alternatives he is evaluating.

Identifying the Buyer's Priorities

The final subject of interest to you is that of the buyer's priorities. Here again, you will have to deal with the problem of the buyer's perception of his situation. Most often, buyers have a few key objectives, such as lowest price or the ability to meet their delivery requirements, that are uppermost on their minds. Finding out that these are top priority is generally not difficult. The rest of his objectives usually fall into a "secondary importance" category, with each of them being seen as having roughly equal weight.

This situation is much to your advantage, for a major part of your sales strategy will involve working with the buyer's priorities so as to shape them in a way that not only reflects his true requirements but also displays your product's performance to maximum advantage. In the fact-finding stage, determining priorities generally poses no difficult problems. Once the buyer has identified a group of objectives, he won't be reluctant to state which are most important to him, and your goal at this stage is merely to learn how clearly he sees his priorities and how firmly he is committed to them. Generally, as we said, the buyer will have a few key objectives and a number of secondary ones. For the fact-finding phase, this separation into "key" and "secondary" is sufficient for your purposes.

The Time Question

As with the opening, the fact-finding phase has no set time limit. Your goal at this point is to develop as much specific information as possible about the ends the buyer is trying to achieve. Depending on the complexity of the situation, a complete and accurate profile may emerge in the first part of a single sales interview or slowly over a number of them. Given your goal, you should impose no artificial time constraints on the fact-finding period, especially since the information you develop during this phase is critical to the next stage in the sales process, strategy development.

FIVE

THE
SALES STRATEGY

Developing an effective sales strategy is a matter of analyzing each aspect of the buyer's decision problem in order to identify your areas of advantage over the competition. This involves four basic steps, all of which draw heavily upon our model of the systematic buying decision:

Analysis of the buyer's criteria.

Evaluation of your product in the light of the buyer's criteria.

Formulation of a plan for improving the fit between these criteria and your product's performance.

Implementation of your sales strategy through a presentation.

More specifically, developing your sales strategy can be seen as answering a series of questions about each of these steps.

Analysis

1. Does the buyer have a *motive* for considering your product?

- Can you show him an *opportunity* to improve his already satisfactory situation?
- Are there areas of *dissatisfaction* that you can respond to?
- Are there any *risks* facing the buyer that might induce him to consider your product?
- If the prospect is considering a competitor's product, what motives has he for doing so?

2. How does the buyer define his *basic goal?* What is he trying to achieve as a result of his purchase?

3. What are the *criteria*—constraints, objectives, and priorities—on which the buyer will base his decision?

Evaluation

1. Do any of the alternatives considered by the buyer not meet his constraints?

2. Are there inherent risks attached to any of the buyer's alternatives?

3. How does each of the alternatives perform against each of the buyer's objectives?

4. Which of the choices provides the best cumulative performance against the buyer's priority-weighted list of objectives?

Formulation of your plan

1. Does your product perform clearly better than the competition in the light of the buyer's criteria? If so, your next step is the presentation.

2. Is your product's performance not clearly superior to that of your competitors' products? If so, can you redesign your product or shape the buyer's criteria (or both) to improve the performance of your product?

- Can your product be redesigned to become more compatible with the buyer's basic goal? Can his goal definition be shaped—either broadened or narrowed—in a way that would benefit your product?
- Can you redesign your product so that it will meet the buyer's constraints? Can his constraints be shaped so as to include your product or exclude the competition?
- Is the buyer overlooking intolerable risks attached to any of the competitors' products?
- Can your product be redesigned to match the buyer's objectives more closely? Can you shape the buyer's perception of any of his objectives, thereby improving your product's performance? Can you suggest additional objectives that would benefit your product?
- Can you redesign your product to improve its fit with the buyer's priorities? Can you reorder the priorities to improve your product's chances?

Implementation

The final step in your sales strategy is to put it to the test of action. This means making a presentation to the buyer in which you demonstrate that your product is the best means to achieve his true ends. Insofar as you found it necessary to redesign your product, this, of course, will have to be completed before the presentation.

ANALYZING THE BUYER'S CRITERIA

The first step in formulating your sales strategy is to examine the information that you gathered during the fact-finding phase and analyze it in terms of the steps of the buying decision process. Some of the buyer's criteria probably are inappropriate for his situation, and you may well find it necessary to shape them. However, at this stage you're merely taking stock; you are trying to get an accurate picture of how the *buyer* views his decision task.

Your basic tool for the analysis again is our model of the systematic buying decision. This means that you proceed from the buyer's *motive* for entering the decision process to his *basic goal* and from there to his specific criteria—his constraints, objectives, and priorities. If you've handled the fact-finding phase well, this part of strategy development will be easy because you will have elicited the relevant information from the buyer with a constant view of its significance to the buying decision.

The details of the analysis do not need to be discussed here; they can be found in the chapter on the initial interview.

EVALUATING YOUR PRODUCT

In order to evaluate your product realistically, you must put yourself in the customer's position and go through the decision process as he would. As we have seen in Chapter One, the evaluation phase of a systematic buying decision comprises four basic steps. First, the available alternatives must be examined as to their compatibility with the buyer's constraints. Second, the choices must be scrutinized as to inherent risks that might prove unacceptable. Third, each product's performance against each objective must be determined. Fourth, the buyer must decide which alternative meets most of his important objectives.

These, then, are the four basic areas of product performance that you must consider. There are two possible outcomes of your evaluation: Either your product emerges as the buyer's best choice, given his own criteria, or your product isn't the best choice as things stand now. In the first case, your next task simply is to communicate to the buyer the logic of choosing your product. You must demonstrate, in other words, that your product indeed meets the buyer's criteria better than the others.

Of course, if buyers made perfectly rational decisions, there would be no need for you to prove that your product is the best choice; the buyer would already know this. But buyers, like people in general, do not always make systematic decisions. More importantly, you cannot *depend* on their making good decisions. Your safest bet is to assume that the buyer will act illogically, and given that logic points to your product as the optimal alternative, you must make sure that the buyer stays on the path of reason.

Exactly how do you do this? Again, by using your understanding of the decision process. The fact that a product is the best choice can best be proved by reconstructing for the buyer the rational steps in the decision process. In other words, the buying decision process provides the method not only of analyzing which is the best product, but also of communicating the logic of the choice. It serves as the means of both developing and implementing the sales strategy.

Good communication is a matter of organizing ideas in a sequence such that the buyer can follow you to the logical conclusion, and the steps in the decision process as we defined them, give you that logical organization. The basic sequence is first to summarize for the buyer the ends he is trying to achieve, then to show him how your product helps him achieve those ends better than any of the other alternatives available.

Formulating Your Sales Plan

Things are relatively easy when your evaluation of the buyer's situation shows that your product is best suited to his purposes. But what if your analysis shows that your product doesn't meet his ends quite as well as does the competition's? Clearly, in that event you have three choices: lose the business, change the product, or change the buyer's criteria.

In most cases losing the business is of course not an acceptable choice. Still, you may run into situations where your own analysis shows that your product is clearly not compatible with a particular prospect's requirements. In that event, you may be about to waste sales time, and it may be in your own best interest to forget about the prospect in question.

In other words, your analysis can help you set some priorities for your accounts. It tells you which ones are most likely to buy your products and which ones are not really good prospects. Time being a limited resource, it is better to invest it in accounts that offer reasonable chance of success than in hopeless causes. Hard as it may seem, sometimes the best sales strategy for a particular account is indeed to forget about it and go on to more promising prospects.

When you do want to pursue the account, however, you are left with two choices:

Changing your product to make it fit the buyer's criteria.

Changing the buyer's criteria to make your product more competitive.

This is not meant to suggest that you must choose strictly between these two approaches. Clearly, in most situations you will want to follow both in order to strengthen the overall fit between your product and the buyer's criteria.

Redesigning Your Product to Improve Its Performance

Earlier we made the point that taking a customer-oriented approach allows a company to be flexible in its product line. As the customers' requirements change, the customer-oriented company modifies its product line to match the new buyer criteria. We also discussed the function of ongoing market research and saw that it helps the company identify buyer criteria as they evolve so that the necessary changes in the products can be initiated. The customer-oriented company always is in a "design" mode; it is continually redesigning its products to match changing buyer criteria. Product-oriented companies, on the other hand, overlook changes in buyer criteria. Consequently, they tend to have static product lines, and the more buyer criteria change, the less competitive their products become.

The same holds true for salesmen. Whereas the customer-oriented salesman is sensitive to changes in his customer's decision situations, the product-oriented salesman memorizes a presentation and repeats it without much regard for the buyer's criteria. That presentation originally may have been appropriate, but as the buyer's needs change, it increasingly loses its effectiveness. Both the product and the presentation must change to keep in tune with buyer requirements. The product-oriented salesman eventually loses because he does not recognize changes in the buyer.

What we're saying, in effect, is that part of the sales function is market research. When a customer-oriented salesman detects changes in the buyer's criteria, it is his responsibility to redesign his product so that it matches the buyer's new criteria. That is the only way for him to stay competitive. But how is the salesman to make these changes? In what way can he redesign his product? The problem becomes especially thorny for the industrial salesman who is offering a commodity or material that is fairly well set. How can he redesign a coil of steel, for instance?

Remember our basic point: A product is a means by which the buyer achieves certain ends. These ends ultimately determine the criteria on which the prospect bases his decision. Buyers invariably use a number of criteria that transcend the mere physical makeup of the product. A moment's reflection will show that any product does indeed have many aspects that are independent of its physical nature and hence may not be fixed at all. A coil of stainless steel, for example, has a basic physical composition that is set. You can't change that composition without changing the very nature of the coil. But it also has a price, which presumably isn't fixed. It has a delivery schedule. It has a weight that can be changed—you can put more or less steel in the coil. It has been manufactured so as to meet certain quality standards. Those standards are not fixed; they may vary depending on the use the buyer has in mind. In short, there are a vast number of aspects to any product which are flexible, and this is true even for products that seem totally unchangeable at first thought.

A product is simply a response to a set of buyer criteria, and those criteria go into the design specifications of the product. Insofar as they concern flexible aspects of the salesman's product, he has the option of trying to change the product accordingly. This, of course, requires the cooperation of his management. The salesman has a market research task in the sense that he must probe for buyer criteria and signal to management any mismatch between product design and market demands. To the extent that he succeeds in this, and to the extent that management is responsive to the information passed on by the salesman, the product can be brought in line with the buyer's criteria to make it more competitive.

To put it differently, the buyer's complete criteria are the specifications used by the salesman to design a competitive *product package* of which the physical makeup of the product—for instance, the steel in a steel coil—is only one part. By keeping alert to the buyer's decision situation, you can continually design product packages that sell, whereas the salesman who ignores the buyer's criteria will ultimately fail, thanks to a static product description. Of course, if your product is intangible—that is, if you're selling a service—changing some of its features is generally easier than if it's tangible.

In attempting to redesign your product, you're again wise to proceed in the sequence defined by the buying decision process. Examine first the possibility of changing the product so that it will match the buyer's basic goal more closely; then consider his constraints and see whether your product can be adjusted to achieve a better fit; then do the same for his objectives and priorities. This procedure can save you much unnecessary work. For instance, it would be futile to redesign your product to improve its performance with respect to one of the buyer's minor objectives when you know for sure that it's impossible to meet one of his important constraints or several of his top-priority objectives.

Changing the Buyer's Criteria

It may seem like a contradiction of our concern with "customer orientation" to suggest that the salesman can—and sometimes should—try to change the criteria on which a prospect bases a buying decision.

There is a difference, however, between being customer-oriented and being customer-controlled. Being customer-oriented means attending to the customer's decision situation before proceeding to the product presentation. It does not necessarily mean that you have to accept as inflexible law everything the prospect says. Nor does it mean that you must stop speaking out for your product or surrender your self-interest to the unalterable will of the prospect.

True, your overall goal should be to develop a quality buying decision that accurately reflects the buyer's requirements; this is in your own interest because it will increase the chance that the customer will buy from you again. But engineering quality decisions is not incompatible with trying to alter the buyer's criteria. In fact, often the salesman can alter the buyer's stated criteria in a way that ultimately is to the buyer's benefit. Just as buyers often make poor decisions, they often set objectives that, if left unchanged, would result in the choice of an alternative hardly suited to their real requirements.

Recall, for instance, our example of the man who decides that his basic goal is to purchase a four-wheel-drive vehicle that is sure to get him up his steep driveway no matter what the weather. As we've seen, his perception of his goal is far from accurate. His real concern is to ensure mobility to and from his house under all weather conditions. There are a number of ways to achieve this; buying a four-wheel-drive vehicle is only one of them. Another solution might be to contract with a snow removal service; still another might be to buy a snowplow or blower. Either of these would get him out of his driveway—at a considerable saving.

Poor criteria-setting on the part of the buyer, then, will lead to poor decisions. Hence it can be perfectly consistent with the philosophy of customer orientation to work with a prospect to reshape his original criteria. Better buying decisions can be the result and, just as importantly, increased sales. To put it differently, buyer and seller are working together to achieve a rational, systematic decision. The buyer has certain ends; the seller has the means. To bring these ends and means together in the best possible match often requires shaping of both the product and the buyer's criteria.

What does it mean to shape the buyer's criteria? Basically, it involves rephrasing a specific criterion or altering the buyer's overall list of criteria in a way that more accurately reflects his requirements and/or improves the performance of the salesman's product. To use another simple example, suppose a man is shopping for a new house in the suburbs. Having to commute to the city, he tells the real estate salesman that his house ideally should be no more than ten minutes from a train station because he wants to keep his commuting time down to, say, one hour at a maximum. Suppose further that although the agent has no listings meeting that particular objective, he does have listed several homes that are located along a suburban bus route into the city. Shaping the buyer's criteria would in this case involve changing his stated objective from "maximally ten minutes from a train station" to "maximally one hour commuting time from the city." Unless the buyer has a strong aversion to buses, his basic requirements will be met, and the salesman may be able to sell him a house that did not measure up at all to his objective as originally stated.

Two related basic facts make it possible for you to shape the prospect's decision criteria: (1) the buyer does not know your product as well as you do, (2) knowing your product's performance, you can judge which buyer criteria it meets best.

To know your product means to know the ideal set of buyer criteria that it was designed to satisfy. That is, there is a set of constraints, objectives, and priorities that your product meets completely and with clear superiority over the competition. Unfortunately, you rarely run into a prospect whose criteria exactly match this ideal set. This is where the need for shaping arises. Your task is to work with the prospect's stated criteria so as to make them fall more closely in line with the ideal list of criteria for your product. The firmer your understanding of this ideal, the clearer your idea of how to shape the prospect's stated criteria.

To put it differently, there is an ideal buyer for each product, someone whose decision situation is answered by the product in every detail. Shaping involves moving an actual prospect as close to the ideal buyer as possible. It means rephrasing actual, or stated, criteria until they match or approximate the ideal buyer's criteria.

Shaping is possible in a service business too, in which there is no product per se. If we can speak of a product here, it is the salesman's expertise, and he knows best what its limits are; he knows his own strong and weak points. To put it in our terminology, he has an ideal buyer in mind, someone whose needs he could answer precisely and better than anybody. His task, then, is the same: to bring the prospect's perception and understanding of his ends into line with those of the ideal buyer.

To know your product, in short, means to understand which ends your product meets best and evaluate its performance from the buyer's perspective. The ability of the salesman to shape a prospect's stated objectives depends on this kind of product knowledge.

Thinking of product knowledge in this way may well be unfamiliar to many salesmen, who consequently will have no "ideal" buyer profile in mind. It is easily developed, however, and once developed, it will remain the same as long as the product is unchanged. The basis for your ideal buyer profile is the set of original design specifications for your product—the constraints and objectives that it achieves. Presumably, there *is* such a set of design specifications, for your product, like any other, was created to achieve certain specific objectives. They are by definition the ideal buyer's objectives, since the perfect buyer for any product is someone who wants to achieve just those ends that the product's original designers were trying to satisfy.

Generally you will not be able to influence the buyer's criteria during the initial sales interview, where your job is to gather information about the ends the prospect is trying to achieve. There are some situations, however, in which on-the-spot shaping is possible. To return to our real estate example, we can imagine the initial conversation to run somewhat as follows:

PROSPECT: Any house I buy will have to be no more than ten minutes from the train station.

SALESMAN: What would be the maximum amount of commuting time you would consider?

PROSPECT: Certainly no more than an hour.

SALESMAN: Well then, can we say that any house you consider should be no more than one hour's commute from the city?

As we said, however, in most cases not much shaping can be done during the initial interview (assuming a two-interview sale) or the initial stages of a single-interview sale. For one thing, if you tell a prospect that your first concern is to learn what he wants to achieve, only to proceed to change each objective he mentions, your sincerity can be called into question. For another, you really *are* interested in the prospect's objectives and perceptions; they play a critical role in your presentation.

Your first goal, therefore, is to collect these bits of data. Later, when analyzing the situation in detail, you can ask yourself how certain criteria might be shaped so as to improve the performance of your product. In other words, shaping more often occurs during your analysis of the prospect and his buying situation than during interaction with him. Of course, in single-interview sales, shaping must occur—if it occurs at all—during the interview, but the basic sequence is the same: Collecting extensive data on the prospect's perception of his criteria generally must precede any attempt to shape specific criteria.

Assuming a multiple-interview sales situation, how can you go about shaping the prospect's criteria as you have understood them from the initial interview? So far, you have categorized all the relevant information according to the buying process, thereby reconstructing the prospect's decision. You know what his motives are for considering the product and how he sees his basic goal, constraints, objectives, and priorities. You also have evaluated the performance of your product in the light of the buyer's criteria, and therefore you know which criteria need to be shaped. What remains to be done is to go through the elements of the buying decision, from motive to priorities, and search for areas in which the buyer's perceptions could be corrected.

There is not much you can do about the prospect's motive for considering your product. He either had a valid motive before you saw him, or else you supplied one for him. This is not meant to imply that the salesman cannot "create" a buying motive out of the information supplied by an uncommitted prospect, but the concept of shaping as we've discussed it is not really applicable to the buyer's motive. With motives, you are simply interested in their *existence*, whereas in the case of the buyer's evaluation criteria you are concerned with their specific *content*.

Turning to the buyer's definition of his basic goal, however, there often are good opportunities for exerting your influence. Recall again the example of the fellow with the steep driveway. His initial definition of his buying decision was to select a four-wheel-drive vehicle. The boundaries of that definition included all the various makes of four-wheel-drive cars. Shaping of that definition, however, so that it reflects the snow-bound buyer's real need—to get up his driveway— allows other alternatives to enter the boundaries, including snowblowers, skimobiles, and snow removal services. They may all turn out to be unsatisfactory once they are evaluated against specific criteria, but one thing is certain: As long as the goal definition is focused on four-wheel-drive cars, these other alternatives would not even be considered. If, as a salesman selling snowblowers you evaluate your products in the light of this narrow definition, you will realize quickly that you must either shape it or be left out in the cold.

To take another simple example, a real estate buyer who says he is looking for a new house may be susceptible to your suggestion that he is really looking for a place to live, and that broader definition would include condominiums, town houses, apartments, even houseboats, all of which fall outside the original narrow definition of his basic goal. Here again, whether you attempt to alter the buyer's perception and how you go about doing it depend on your evaluation of your products. If you have nothing but houses in your listings, there obviously is no point in trying to shape your prospect's basic definition. If, on the other hand, you have a number of condominiums you need to move, changing the prospect's definition might be useful.

Similarly, the buyer's constraints can be shaped in a way that may benefit the salesman and eliminate a competitor. Suppose, for instance, that you're selling industrial chemicals, in particular, a dry chemical which has been used by a certain customer for some time now. Its disadvantage is that it requires mixing at the site. However, the customer is set up for this process and has been using it successfully for many years. A salesman from a competing company is trying to break into the account. His product is a liquid. It has the same chemical formula as your product, but because it isn't in dry form it is somewhat easier to handle. In particular, it requires no mixing and therefore reduces labor costs. It is also cleaner: There are none of the dust problems that occur when the dry formula is transported or dumped into mixing hoppers. In order to use the liquid product, however, the customer must install large storage tanks and feed lines. Your competitor's company is willing to underwrite the cost of these tanks, however, so switching to the liquid form would not cost the customer any money.

Although at first, things may look bad for your product, you may be able to save the account. For instance, you may be informed about severe storage limitations. In that case, you obviously would point out to the customer that any product he considers must meet his space constraints, which would eliminate the possibility of introducing your competitor's storage tanks. No matter what the advantages of the liquid product, the customer is barred from considering it as long as space is a limiting factor. Assuming the customer accepts this constraint as valid, the situation becomes very difficult for your competitor, for he finds himself outside the limits that the buyer has established.

Note that the space constraint was never important either to you or your customer until your competitor arrived on the scene; implicitly, however, it always existed, and you knew about it because you took care to analyze the customer's situation thoroughly. Shaping, in this case, meant highlighting a constraint that the customer was likely to accept as a valid limitation on the range of chemical products he could consider.

After constraints, the next area in which you may want to correct the prospect's perceptions is that of unacceptable risks. Such risks, as we have seen, eliminate the product in question from further consideration. As a general rule, therefore, the salesman uses risk criteria strictly to gain an edge over the competition. There may be exceptional instances when he discusses the risks of one of his own products (say, in order to provide better service to an account and thereby solidify the relationship), but in general risk is something attached to *other* products.

Obviously, a risk that the buyer doesn't perceive will not affect his decision. It is therefore your task—and opportunity—to help the buyer identify and evaluate risks that might otherwise go unnoticed. If you're successful in this, you may have introduced a new criterion that changes the very basis on which the prospect's buying decision will be made.

To illustrate our point, consider again the example of the two industrial chemicals salesmen. Suppose that your competitor, who sold the liquid formula, managed to avoid elimination by the customer's severe space limitation by proposing to build a special all-weather outdoor tank. Having survived this test, his next problem is to find a competitive edge over you. He might well exploit the area of unacceptable risks by pointing out to the customer that the new Occupational Safety and Health Act (OSHA) is taking a firm stand on the problem of chemical dust in the air and that continued use of your dry product could cause his entire operation to come under government scrutiny because of the health dangers to the workers. His position is even stronger if he can show that some plants in similar situations were forced to shut down until they solved the dust problem.

Your competitor, in short, would be introducing a risk that is attached to your product but that the buyer had not previously perceived. Whether the risk is unacceptable or not is up to the buyer to judge. If he decides that he cannot run the risk, your company, which is selling the dry chemical, may well be out of the running.

An important point to note in this connection is that buyers tend to be blind to risks attached to products that they have been using for a long time with good results. Having had no problems in the past, they're prejudiced in their old products' favor and therefore likely to forget about things that could go wrong. Also, times change, and while at the time of the original purchase there may not have been any significant risks attached to the product, it may well have acquired them in the meantime, as in our case of the dry chemical conflicting with the new OSHA regulations. Similarly, buyers will tend to overlook possible risks if the product offers them unusual benefits, such as a very low price. Finally, if the buyer is under pressure from management to get a project under way, he will tend to shortcut a careful consideration of the risks that might accompany the product he selects.

If as a salesman for a competing product you find such a situation, where you're able to identify certain unperceived risks attached to your competitor's products, you stand a good chance to win the account. Perhaps you cannot come up with a risk that disqualifies the competition, but it is likely to play some role in the buyer's decision because it will be transformed into an objective in his mind. Avoiding the risk that you pointed out, in other words, will become one of his objectives.

Having considered the problem of shaping the buyer's constraints and sharpening his awareness of potential risks, your next step is to examine his objectives. There are two things you may be able to do in this area: (1) alter a specific stated objective to improve the performance of your product in the buyer's eyes, and (2) introduce new objectives, thereby changing the buyer's overall list of criteria in your favor.

To illustrate the first technique—changing a specific objective—let us return once more to our industrial chemicals example. The buyer naturally will have some objective with regard to delivery, and being used to receiving frequent deliveries of the dry chemical, which he cannot store in large quantities, one of his objectives might be to have guaranteed regular deliveries. The salesman selling the liquid product can meet that objective as well as his competitor, who sells the dry powder. However, by shaping the buyer's objective, he can gain an advantage and improve the performance of his product with regard to this particular concern of the buyer.

The outside liquid storage tanks, we have said, have a very great capacity, and because of this, there's need for only two or three deliveries a year. Keeping this in mind, the salesman may attempt to revise the buyer's original objective to that of ongoing guaranteed availability. Obviously, this is the buyer's real concern: He doesn't want to run out of materials. As long as he is thinking in terms of deliveries, there is virtually no difference between the two products, but by focusing on what the buyer really wants to achieve and relating it to his own product knowledge, the salesman can shape the buyer's criteria in a way that gives him a competitive edge. His liquid does a better job of achieving ongoing guaranteed availability simply because it requires fewer deliveries. It is in place at the plant in the storage tank and therefore is less susceptible to delivery problems.

The second technique for shaping objectives, namely introducing additional ones, is straightforward. You've learned from the buyer what he is trying to achieve as a result of his purchase. In analyzing his criteria, and specifically the objectives, you may notice that he has omitted one that your product is well designed to meet. Chances are that the buyer will accept the additional objective, to the extent that he has the same general ends in mind that originally led to the product's design.

To stay with our industrial chemicals example, the salesman selling the liquid product might suggest that the buyer should be interested in reducing labor costs. The buyer will certainly not disagree with that objective, despite the fact that he did not mention it himself. With respect to this new objective, the liquid, which requires no handling, easily outperforms the dry substance, which must be mixed by hand.

Your final step is to consider the buyer's priorities, with a view to opportunities for shaping them. Setting priorities, more perhaps than anything else, is an exercise in judgment. Consequently, priorities tend to be the most flexible aspect of the decision-making process. They are also nearly always the key factor determining the outcome of the decision process.

Buyers, as we have seen, generally have only one or two very important objectives and a number of others that they consider less important. In other words, they tend to divide their objectives into two general categories, critical and secondary, and generally the final decision is based on the buyer's assessment of which product achieves his *critical* objectives best. It is not unheard of that a buyer selects a product that performs poorly against his critical objectives but is clearly superior in all secondary ones: The cumulative effect may just make it the overall best choice. However, this is a rare situation indeed. In most cases, buyers will choose those products or services which outperform the competition with respect to the buyer's critical objectives while performing perhaps no more than adequately in secondary areas. Of course, the more similar competing products are in terms of satisfying critical objectives, the more important secondary objectives become. In such a situation, secondary, even trivial, objectives may well become the means of choosing between two evenly matched products.

Buyers, then, if they think about priorities at all, do not go to the trouble of identifying which is top, which second, which third, and so on, but tend to say simply, "These are key—these aren't, but I'd like to achieve them if I can." This practice, which seems to be almost automatic, is of course in line with one of our basic premises, that buyers often do not make very good or careful decisions. This offhanded approach to priority setting offers you excellent opportunities for influencing the buying decision.

Clearly, it should be far easier to modify the priorities of a prospect who has not carefully thought about them than of someone who has established a detailed hierarchy of objectives. It is essential that you exercise your influence in this respect whenever possible, for as we have said, the buyer will ultimately select the product that best meets the objectives most important in his eyes. Once you have appropriately adjusted the buyer's perception of his own priorities, demonstrating that your product meets the important objectives better than the competition should be a straightforward matter.

But how do you go about shaping a prospect's priorities? By applying your expertise, your intimate knowledge of the product and the market. Suppose again you're the industrial chemicals salesman trying to break into an account with a new liquid product. Suppose, further, that you know about a probable shortage of raw materials in the coming year and that your company has been farsighted enough to secure adequate amounts of its materials to be able to guarantee its customers a continuous supply even during a shortage. Maintaining a continuous supply obviously is one of the buyer's critical objectives, but by raising the question of the shortage, you can bring it to the center of his attention, and in all probability it will take on overriding importance, more so than quality and price, which are other common critical objectives. If your company can give better supply guarantees than your competitor, you will most likely get the business, assuming that the two products are comparable in all other objectives.

Looking at the problem from the point of view of your competitor, he obviously should try to shift the buyer's focus away from the supply objective to another of the "criticals," for instance, price. He might respond as follows:

> "It's true, we anticipate a supply squeeze, and the resultant decrease in supply, combined with constant demand, will undoubtedly shoot the price sky-high. In fact, some companies will be forced into red-ink situations because of the cost of materials. In order to alleviate this problem for good customers, however, we are willing to give you a year-long contract price."

Such an approach may well succeed in turning the buyer's attention from the supply theme to the price objective and so, in effect, alter his perception of his priorities.

How realistic is all this? Is it actually possible to shape a buyer's criteria in the way we have suggested? Clearly, it is not feasible to revamp every one of them. In the first place, buyers would obviously resent what they would correctly regard as an attempt at improper manipulation. Nor is such an aggressively manipulative approach in your own interest: It is inconsistent with the philosophy of developing quality buying decisions. If you alter all of the buyer's criteria to sell your product, you probably are not serving the buyer's best interests. At some point in the future he will realize that he made a bad decision, that is, that the product does not meet his real requirements, and that will be the end of his relationship with you.

On the other hand, it is usually possible to shape one or two objectives or alter the buyer's perception of his constraints or his priorities in a way that reflects and protects his true interests while at the same time improving your product's performance vis-à-vis the competition. In other words, you may have only a few opportunities in any sales situation to shape the buyer's criteria, but they will often make the difference, especially when two or more products are in close competition.

SALES VERSUS MARKETING

It may be useful to make a comparison here between the sales function and marketing. Both, after all, are concerned with the finding and keeping of customers for a company's products. In marketing, the first step is to conduct research into what buyers want, the next, to develop or change the product according to the results of that research. That task completed, advertising and promotion are used to shape the market's buying criteria—that is, its perception of its own wants. Where necessary, buyer criteria may be *created* through appropriate use of attitude-forming media. The last task for the marketing function is to communicate the idea to buyers that their wants are best satisfied by the product.

The sales function faces analogous tasks. The major difference is that as a salesman you deal with comparatively few buyers, whereas marketing is directed at large numbers of people. Of necessity, marketing uses techniques for gathering mass information, and the mass media are its means of communicating with the buyers. Salesmen, on the other hand, deal with individual buyers and individual companies. Even where several people have an impact on the ultimate decision, they are still few compared to the numbers involved in marketing. Also, marketing can effectively create and change buyer criteria through the use of propaganda media. As a salesman you cannot really mold opinion in this way. Yet, the basic similarity between marketing and sales remains: Both are directed toward creating buyers. The basic process underlying sales and marketing can be summarized in this figure:

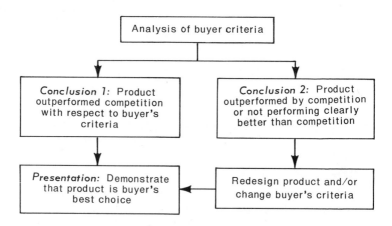

THE SALES STRATEGY ILLUSTRATED

A hypothetical case will illustrate how to use our model of the buying decision process to formulate an effective sales strategy.

A vice president of a large textile company—the Sixstar Textiles Company—is sitting in his New York office flipping through a trade journal. He comes across an advertisement that is directed toward textile producers. It announces that sodium hydrosulfite can now be bought for 30¢ a pound. The vice president is annoyed; his company currently buys the chemical from another supplier, paying well over 40¢ a pound. Sodium hydrosulfite is used as a bleaching agent, and since all the textiles this company manufactures go through a bleaching process at some point, it is essential to its operations. Indeed, Sixstar Textiles uses sodium hydrosulfite in such quantities that a saving of more than 10¢ per pound would get to be very meaningful over a year's period. The vice president calls his plant and tells the purchasing agent to look into the advertised 30¢ product.

Sodium hydrosulfite is a compound that can be produced by a number of processes. Acme Chemicals, the company offering the 30¢ product, actually isn't offering a finished chemical but rather a process that can be used by textile companies to produce sodium hydrosulfite at a cost of roughly 30¢ per pound. The process involves installing fairly complex equipment for blending the various ingredients. The cost of the installation is in the neighborhood of $200,000, but that money can be regarded as a good investment insofar as it would allow the textile company to save over 25 percent on a critical basic material.

There is a catch. The new process depends on a certain chemical that is produced exclusively by Acme. Without that chemical, the process offered by Acme is useless.

The purchasing agent at the textile plant calls Acme Chemicals to learn about the advertised 30¢ product. After obtaining the necessary information he talks with the worried salesman from Edgworth Chemicals, currently Sixstar's principal supplier of sodium hydrosulfite. In effect, he is saying, "I'm looking into the 30¢ hydrosulfite from Acme. We're now paying you 43¢ a pound, but since we've had a good relationship in the past, I want to give you a chance to respond to this development." What he is asking, of course, is whether Edgworth can meet Acme's price.

To Edgworth, the situation seems clear and simple: either cut the price or lose the business. In other words, the company defines its problem as whether or not to lower its price. That decision has no happy alternatives. A substantial price cut would severely reduce the profit from the Sixstar account. As a matter of fact, if Edgworth tried to meet Acme's price, it would lose money. As Edgworth sees it, losing the business is the only other option, and that clearly holds few attractions.

In fact, however, the decision Edgworth should wrestle with is not whether to cut the price. Rather, the company should focus on the buyer's decision. A closer analysis of Sixstar's situation would give management a good idea of the optimal strategy for dealing with this particular account.

The first thing Edgworth needs to consider is the textile company's motivation for considering new ways of securing sodium hydrosulfite. Sixstar evidently was not dissatisfied with Edgworth's prior work, nor was it facing risks by staying with Edgworth as its principal supplier. Rather, the textile company saw an opportunity to improve an already satisfactory situation, namely a chance to reduce costs by switching to Acme's process for producing sodium hydrosulfite. Sixstar may not be motivated to actually *buy* Acme's product; but the company certainly is motivated to investigate the situation.

Looking at it from this point of view, the purchasing agents at Sixstar clearly were doing the right thing; they had a valid motive for reevaluating the company's situation. It would therefore be pointless and possibly self-defeating for the Edgworth sales people to try to dissuade the textile buyers from undertaking the reevaluation. There is no hope of success in trying to persuade someone not to do something that is clearly in his best interest.

Having identified the reason for Sixstar Textiles' interest in considering a new buying decision, Edgworth's next step should be to determine what the textile company's decision is all about. Note that Edgworth's competitor, Acme, has been particularly clever in this, for it has, in effect, shown Sixstar that the textile company's problem is not where to buy hydrosulfite but how to acquire the necessary supply. This expanded definition allows Acme, which does not produce hydrosulfite, to become a valid alternative.

Here again, the textile company is doing the proper thing. There is not a chance that Edgworth could convince Sixstar to revert to its original narrower goal definition. What's more, there is no need to try, since Edgworth is still a valid alternative under the new definition. By broadening Sixstar's definition of its basic goal Acme cleverly injected itself as a legitimate alternative, but it did not eliminate Edgworth—or any other competitor, for that matter.

Edgworth's next step in analyzing Sixstar's decision situation should be to consider the constraints within which the textile company must work. There is sure to be a budget constraint of some kind, but it cannot have an impact on the problem at hand since both Edgworth and Acme are well within the budget limits, Edgworth having sold at a previously acceptable price and Acme having bid below that figure. Thus the absolute limits of Sixstar's budget are not violated by either competitor. Edgworth, consequently, cannot outperform Acme on the basis of Sixstar's constraints.

Still, it is well worth the time to analyze the client's constraints because if Edgworth's salesman can identify a constraint that the client has overlooked and that his competitor cannot meet, he may be able to eliminate the competitor. For instance, if Acme's process requires massive amounts of storage and production space beyond what is available to the textile company, Acme would be out of the running despite its attractive price. As we've seen, an alternative that falls outside the decision makers constraints can no longer be considered.

This again illustrates the advantages of customer orientation. Instead of trying to outshout or outdazzle the competition in describing his products, the salesman can often win by looking at the situation from the customer's perspective. The key point here is that customers may forget to consider their own constraints, but the salesman should not.

In the next step, Edgworth must consider Sixstar's objectives. Often buyers concentrate on one or two key objectives at the expense of others that may be equally important. Buyers, in other words, will be more inclined to say, "My objective *is* . . ." than "My objectives *are* . . ." This tendency is reinforced in a situation such as Sixstar's because the opportunity to save money tends to direct the focus entirely on price. From Acme's point of view, this is a positive situation, for if the textile company bases its decision solely on what company can provide the cheapest sodium hydrosulfite, Acme will win. Edgworth, however, should realize that Sixstar has other objectives as well, and Edgworth's ability to achieve these better than Acme might have the cumulative effect of tipping the decision in Edgworth's favor. But it is up to Edgworth to identify these additional objectives because here again, the company cannot afford to rely on the buyer to do it.

In our example, this problem is related to that of setting priorities. By concentrating on the price objective, the buyer is saying that low price is his top, if not his only, objective. But again, he may be overlooking certain factors that are actually more important to him than low price. For instance, Sixstar should also worry about regular deliveries, quality, availability, and so on, and these objectives might very well be more important than price. By pointing these out to the buyer, the Edgworth salesman could overcome Acme's initial superiority. On the other hand, if Edgworth fails to identify these additional objectives and priorities, it will certainly lose because Sixstar's decision in that case will be made on the single price objective.

Let us assume, however, that after identifying all of Sixstar's objectives and arranging them in an accurate priority, Edgworth still appears to have no noticeable edge over Acme. There's still no reason to give up. Rather, Edgworth should proceed to take a closer look at the process of *evaluating* the two alternatives—again from the buyer's perspective.

The first step in evaluation is to determine whether the alternatives meet the buyer's constraints. As we have already seen, both Edgworth and Acme do, and therefore neither can use this means of eliminating the other.

The next thing to consider is whether there are any unacceptable risks attached to any of the alternatives. And this is the area on which Edgworth can base its sales strategy, for there are some very real risks facing the textile company if it decides to use Acme's process. Most important, Sixstar would be tying itself down to a single supplier. Recall that Acme's process for producing sodium hydrosulfite is dependent on a specific ingredient that is produced only by this company; without it, the process will not work. Sixstar therefore runs the risk of spending $200,000 to install the equipment required for Acme's process, only to find itself, at some point in the future, without sodium hydrosulfite, a chemical, as we saw, that is essential to their operation. All that is needed is a strike at Acme or a problem due to materials shortages at that company, or any of a number of reasons that could interrupt the supply of Acme's ingredient.

Of course, if such a situation did occur, Sixstar might go back to its former suppliers of sodium hydrosulfite for interim supplies. But Edgworth could point out that generally plant capacity is fairly well sold, and that it may take the old suppliers some time to locate backup suppliers. Needless to say, delays in operation are tremendously costly.

On the other hand, if Sixstar were to stay with Edgworth as its principal supplier of sodium hydrosulfite, the risk of shortages and shutdowns is not eliminated; it is only greatly reduced. There have never been delivery problems in the past, and there is no particular reason to expect any. Furthermore, even if Edgworth were hit by a strike, Sixstar could turn to minor suppliers for interim shipments, and these would be happy to accommodate the textile company in order to increase their share of the business.

In the face of the risks inherent in introducing a new process that is unfamiliar to Sixstar and totally dependent on a single supplier for its continued viability, Sixstar should think twice before abandoning the previously satisfactory supplier relationship with Edgworth. Making this clear to Sixstar essentially is the sales strategy that Edgworth can adopt to defeat Acme. At the very least, the company now has a strong story to tell, whereas before, it was agonizing over the problem of whether to cut its price or lose the business. By focusing on the buyer's decision, Edgworth has a good chance to salvage a situation that initially seemed hopeless.

In this example, then, there seems to be no need to redesign the product. Rather, the appropriate strategy for Edgworth is to change the buyer's criteria, in particular, to draw his attention to an unacceptable risk attached to the competition's product.

REDESIGNING YOUR PRODUCT ILLUSTRATED

As we have said, when evaluating your product in the light of the buyer's criteria, you may come to the conclusion that in order to beat the competition, you must redesign your product in certain ways. Naturally, this tends to be easier in service businesses than when you're selling tangible products. The following hypothetical case, which deals with the sale of advertising space, will illustrate some of the strategic planning involved in redesigning a product or service.

The prospect in this case is ARG, a large producer of replacement glass for cars and trucks. The salesman trying to win this account represents *Insurance Review*, a magazine aimed at the insurance industry. His goal is to persuade ARG to buy advertising space in his magazine.

At the time of the salesman's first call, ARG is advertising in a competing magazine. The company never advertised in *Insurance Review*, largely because the salesman who handled the account previously for some reason showed little interest in it. At the same time, the salesman from *Insurance Review*'s main competitor spent quite a bit of time on ARG, with the result that ARG is spending a considerable amount of money for advertising in his magazine.

At first glance, the fact that ARG advertises in *any* insurance magazine might seem hard to justify since it doesn't sell to the insurance industry. Its market is independent auto glass replacement outlets—repair shops that specialize in replacing damaged auto glass and consequently must buy their stock from large manufacturers such as ARG.

The insurance industry is important to ARG, however, because insurance agents provide 90 percent of the referrals to the repair shops. Generally, agents do not require their clients to get a number of bids. Knowing most of the repair shops, the agents know which are competitively priced and likely to provide the client with fast, easy service.

Thus, the insurance agent is important to the repair shops, and since the repair shops are important to ARG, ARG supports them with advertising in the insurance trade press. The goal of the advertising is to promote ARG glass as a quality product, in the hope that agents will recommend shops that specialize in handling ARG products. ARG knows that realistically, the best it can hope for is to avoid negative attitudes among the agents. Still, this is sufficient justification for spending a certain amount of money on such advertising.

The problem for the salesman from *Insurance Review* is that ARG's advertising objectives are relatively fuzzy. It is trying to reach the insurance agents and convince them that its glass is a quality product. That message can be conveyed through a variety of media, and there seems to be no particular reason to choose *Insurance Review*.

The *Insurance Review* salesman's initial input from the account confirmed this difficulty. In answer to his questions about the criteria on which ARG bases its advertising decisions, he is told that it is primarily a matter of numbers: cost of reaching each thousand readers, circulation, number of readers who handle auto claims, and so on. Since *Insurance Review*'s circulation figures and costs are not superior to those of the competition, the magazine has no clear advantage with respect to these stated objectives.

ARG also wants to advertise in a magazine with high editorial quality, but here again, *Insurance Review* has no clear edge over the competition. In any event, editorial quality is a difficult concept to measure, and the salesman would therefore have a difficult time demonstrating his magazine's superiority in this respect.

However, the buyer at ARG also indicates that one of his most important objectives is to keep up to date on trends and changes in the insurance industry. This information is particularly useful to him in his own marketing plans. He speaks of "ancillary services" that an insurance magazine could provide and states that the availability of such services is of prime concern to him. That is one of the major reasons why he bought advertising space in *Insurance Review*'s competitor, whose salesman was careful to supply ARG with any and all insurance industry information that might have a bearing on ARG's business.

That basically is the information gathered by the salesman during the first interview with ARG's buyer. His next task is to analyze that information and develop his sales strategy.

His analysis is based on a reconstruction of ARG's buying decision. His first step, then, is to identify ARG's motive for entering the decision process. What would cause this company to consider a proposal from

Insurance Review? Why should it even listen to the salesman? What could convince management that there might be some benefit in beginning the decision process again?

It seems clear that ARG is not dissatisfied with its current situation. In fact, the company seems perfectly happy with the services it is receiving from *Insurance Review*'s competitor. Just as clearly, ARG is not facing any risks by not investigating other advertising media. Realistically, the replacement glass company could stop *all* of its insurance advertising without feeling any immediate negative effects. Because its advertising objectives are long-term and general, it is impossible to point out risks inherent in its current handling of advertising.

That leaves only one category of motivation: opportunity. If ARG is not dissatisfied with the current situation and if there are no risks facing the company, the only reason for management to listen to the salesman for *Insurance Review* is if he can show that there is an opportunity to improve its already satisfactory situation.

Clearly, the salesman's job isn't easy. His product doesn't seem to offer any spectacular opportunities. While it is a high-quality magazine, it is not appreciably superior to its competitors as far as its circulation and profile of its readership go. So what can he do?

There seems to be only one solution: He must look elsewhere for that attractive opportunity that would motivate the buyer to reevaluate his situation.

The answer to the salesman's problem lies in the buyer's concern for "ancillary services," that is, information about the insurance industry that could support his own marketing efforts. As it happens, the publisher of *Insurance Review* also publishes a number of books and studies of interest to the industry. The key factor is the depth of *Insurance Review*'s insurance expertise, as manifested not only by the magazine itself but also by the other publishing activities of the parent company. Our salesman could, with perfect validity, claim to represent a resource of information about the insurance industry, and insofar as the ARG buyer is interested in that information, he may be motivated to investigate *Insurance Review* further. He may not be motivated to buy, but at least he will be motivated to evaluate the potential purchase.

The salesman's next step is to define ARG's basic goal. What is the company really trying to achieve? When he first made contact with ARG, he assumed that it was trying to decide on its advertising medium, specifically, which magazine to use. This assumption is natural because the salesman is selling advertising space. Defining the customer's decision in this way, however, creates problems for him, for as we have already indicated, ARG is content with its current advertising, and there are no criteria by which *Insurance Review* is demonstrably superior to the competition.

Under these circumstances, the salesman's next move is to examine the buyer's definition of his basic goal to see whether it can be shaped in ways that would benefit him. And at that point it becomes clear that ARG is not so much interested in advertising as in useful aids in marketing its product. In particular, the company wants what it calls "ancillary services," namely information.

The salesman originally motivated the buyer to listen to him by pointing out the availability of such ancillary services. It is only natural to apply this idea to redefining the buyer's basic goal. ARG's goal is not to select an advertising medium but rather to select the best means of gaining a full range of insurance industry information services. Under this definition, ARG would be buying an association with an information service company, and the price it would pay is in terms of advertising placed in the insurance magazine.

Having carefully analyzed the buyer's decision problem, the salesman now is in a position to redesign his product to make it more competitive. A product-oriented salesman might simply have made his standard advertising presentation and promptly have run into the insuperable obstacle of the buyer's satisfaction with his current advertising program.

The salesman now has three more tasks. First he must specify the buyer's criteria for selecting his optimal source of insurance information. Next he must return to his management to mobilize the appropriate services on ARG's behalf. This is not too difficult, for it involves no more than collecting mailing lists and proprietary publications that would be useful to ARG. The salesman's third step is to respond to ARG with a proposal stating:

- The motive for considering *Insurance Review*.
- The definition of the buyer's basic goal, namely, selection of a company providing a full range of insurance industry information.
- Specific criteria related to this basic goal.
- Additional advertising criteria as originally stated by ARG.
- An outline of how association with *Insurance Review* achieves all these criteria, with accompanying proof, including the mailing lists and additional publications.

In summary, the salesman in our example may be able to sell advertising space to ARG by concentrating on the buyer's decision problem and redesigning his product according to ARG's specifications. No actual changes in the salesman's product are required; it is merely a matter of exploiting the magazine's expertise in the areas of interest to the buyer.

SIX

THE PRESENTATION

In the presentation, you implement your sales strategy. Your purpose at this stage is to make clear to the buyer that your product is his best, most reasonable choice. In addition, the presentation is designed to elicit the buyer's commitment to his decision.

An important point to keep in mind is that the more complex a situation, the less receptive a buyer will be to persuasion, or "pressure" from the salesman. The reason is clear: The more complex the situation, the greater the number of factors the buyer must evaluate in order to make the best decision. In such situations, advocacy of your product must depend on logic rather than persuasion. The emphasis, in short, must be on organization of information, clarity, and logic in order to achieve good communication and make the strongest possible case for your product.

The sales presentation, therefore, is concerned with transmitting information in a way that relies on logic to advocate a particular course of action, namely buying your product. The best way to organize the data that you hope will lead to a purchase of your product is to reconstruct the buying decision step by step. Just as in the fact-gathering phase, where the decision process provided a model for receiving information, so in the presentation phase it provides a model for transmitting information to the buyer. The salesman's detailed steps in the presentation, therefore, are as follows:

- Motivating the buyer to consider a purchase in your product area.
- Defining the buyer's basic goal.
- Identifying the buyer's criteria—his constraints, objectives, and priorities.
- Identifying the product or service that you're selling.
- Evaluating your product in terms of the buyer's criteria and supplying supporting data, including data on risks attached to different products.
- Discussing benefits of your product or service.
- Responding to objections.
- Closing.

We will examine each of these steps individually.

MOTIVATION

Your first step in the presentation is to refocus or sharpen the buyer's perception of his motive for entering the buying-decision process in the first place. From the salesman's point of view it might be perfectly clear why the buyer should listen to his presentation, and it may have been clear to the buyer at one time. But the buyer's perception of an *opportunity* or *risk* or *dissatisfaction* that would direct him toward your product may have faded. At any rate, the salesman should not assume that the buyer's motivation is sufficient. Therefore his first step in the presentation is to refocus the buyer's attention on his reasons for listening to the salesman.

Once again, there are three categories of basic situations in which a buyer should begin the decision process:

1. When he sees an *opportunity* to improve an already satisfactory situation.
2. When he is *dissatisfied* with his current *situation*.
3. When he sees a *risk* that his current situation may deteriorate.

In the presentation the salesman needs to identify specifically which of these motives exist and provide whatever supporting data are required to document his claims. In most cases this need not—and indeed should not—be a long, drawn-out analysis; its only purpose is, after all, to refocus the buyer's attention on his own situation and requirements.

To use an example dealing with health insurance, we can imagine the insurance salesman saying:

"The last time we got together we talked about the way health care costs were skyrocketing—the way they've practically tripled over the past couple of years—and based on that you asked me to take a look at your current major medical coverage."

In this case the salesman is focusing the buyer's attention on the *risk* that with rising health care costs his current major medical insurance may not be adequate to cover cases of protracted illness. Note that it is not necessary to identify the motive *explicitly* as a risk. The three categories of motives are useful to the salesman in cataloging and organizing information about the buyer; but as long as the specific nature of the risk—in our example, inadequate coverage—is clearly perceived by the buyer, there's no need to attach a category label to it.

Of course, this involves a good deal of personal judgment. The salesman may be certain that the buyer is acutely aware of his own motives for entering the decision process, and in such cases it may seem redundant or artificial to repeat the motive. Generally, however, the buyer's perception is not as strong as the salesman would wish, and it is therefore a good idea to start the presentation with a quick review of the specific nature of the opportunities, dissatisfactions, or risks facing the buyer. This is especially true in cases where the salesman had to supply a motive during the first stage of contact with the buyer.

In more complex situations it may be necessary to separate the motivation step from the rest of the presentation. For example, a consulting company selling services in video development might propose a contract with a major business information publisher. The consulting company would take the publisher's existing products and translate them into a video cassette format for eventual distribution by the publisher's sales force. Clearly, the publisher's motive for considering this arrangement is the *opportunity* to expand its business into new areas and media.

At first glance, the opportunity might seem very attractive, and consequently, the salesman should have no problems in the fact-finding stage. Now, his job is to prove that the opportunity is indeed real and to document its extent. The proof would no doubt involve gathering supporting data on the potential market for the cassettes as well as other pertinent information about the precise nature of the opportunity.

In this example, then, the first phase of the salesman's presentation would concentrate solely on demonstrating the existence and extent of a motive for considering his product. This would be followed by a separate stage in which the salesman analyzes the buyer's more specific criteria and the ways in which his product could meet them. In short, the salesman in this case must first educate the buyer in order to strengthen his perception of a motive for entering the decision process. Having done this, the rest of the presentation follows logically.

Defining the Basic Goal

Once the salesman has "motivated" the prospect, his next step in the presentation is to define the buyer's basic goal. Besides focusing the buyer's attention on his decision problem, this points the way to the constraints and objectives (which, in a way, are refinements of his basic goal) that the buyer must consider.

Very often the definition of the buyer's basic goal is understood from the first moment of contact and undergoes no real change during the sales process. A buyer of steel tubing, for example, is basically trying to obtain a supply of that material. As he interacts with various salesmen, the definition of his basic goal will not undergo alteration. In the presentation, it is therefore unnecessary for the salesman to place great emphasis on restating the buyer's basic goal. He already knows it, and identifying it adds little or nothing to the strength of the presentation.

In cases where the buyer's goal definition has undergone some change, on the other hand, it is extremely important for the salesman to define very carefully his perception of the buyer's basic goal. Because the basic goal is the rationale for everything that follows, it is vital that both buyer and seller understand it clearly and agree on its definition.

The most common situation of this kind arises

when the salesman has shaped the buyer's definition. As we have seen in the chapter discussing the sales strategy, it is often possible to alter the buyer's evaluation criteria—including his basic goal—in ways that improve the sales chances of your product. Clearly, if such shaping is to be effective, the buyer must agree with the altered definition of his basic goal. Very often—in fact almost always—you can secure the buyer's agreement simply by stating in what way you have redefined the basic goal and by documenting your reasons for doing so. Obviously, you must work within the limits of probability. You can't sell acids to a caustic soda buyer by telling him that he is really trying to buy chemicals. But you probably would be able to get his agreement if you state that his true goal is to select appropriate materials for neutralizing acids, and in this way you will have included substitutes for caustic soda in the scope of his decision. The new definition makes sense, it is logical.

Getting the buyer's agreement to a shaped goal definition is made easier by the fact that you are presenting it from the standpoint of his own interests. You are saying to him that you have some new insights into his situation that might improve his ability to achieve his own goals. This gives you an edge over the salesman whose basic attitude is: "Let me tell you about my product."

You also have a certain amount of expertise, knowledge of the industry and the different products on the market, and this tends to give you some credibility in the eyes of the buyer.

Finally, whenever possible, you should have information proving the validity of your view of the buyer's goal. The purpose of these data is to demonstrate that the proposed definition is a feasible, reasonable way for the buyer to look at his own situation. Such proof is superfluous where the reasonableness of the altered definition is self-evident, as in our caustic soda example. In other cases, however, it may not be clear to the buyer that it is reasonable to think of his own basic goal in a different way.

For example, as an insurance agent, you may want to sell an ordinary life policy to a prospect whose initial idea was simply to get some inexpensive term insurance coverage. Your task, then, is to expand the prospect's goal definition to something like "building financial security" from the more restrictive "selecting term insurance coverage." Getting the prospect to agree to the definition may not be easy. At the very least you can expect a certain resistance.

Your problem, therefore, is to rationalize the change from the standpoint of the prospect's concerns and interests. You can do this by pointing out that his interest in term coverage is really the result of a *prior decision* on his part—probably one that was made without much careful consideration. Term insurance, in other words, is not so much a basic goal as it is one alternative means by which the real goal—financial security—can be achieved. The prospect probably settled on the term insurance alternative because it was ostensibly the cheapest. Your point is that by concentrating on the real, original goal—financial security—both you and the prospect will be able to examine *all* available alternatives from the standpoint of his objectives and specified limits to select the best.

At this point, you might want to undercut any further resistance by demonstrating that other alternatives, such as ordinary life policies, can be just as inexpensive as term insurance when viewed from the standpoint of their return on investment and the possibilities of borrowing against them. You mention such data here merely to support your contention that the expanded goal definition is more reasonable from the prospect's point of view, and thereby to get the prospect's agreement. Since your recommendation is made from the perspective of the prospect's interests and since it is clearly not in conflict with his needs, there should be no difficulty in gaining the agreement you seek.

Just as a definition can be broadened, as in our last example, so it can be narrowed, and it is in cases like these that proof data can be essential. Using once more the example of the caustic soda buyer, suppose a caustic soda salesman found that a customer changed his goal definition so as to include pH-adjusting chemicals other than caustic soda. Clearly, if the salesman were able to narrow the goal definition again, he could eliminate his competitor's substitute products. To do this, he needs to document the contention that these substitutes are not as effective as caustic soda and therefore are not true substitutes. If such data were available, the salesman could make an effective case for a narrowed definition, that is, for the idea that the buyer's decision problem is to select a source of caustic soda.

Similarly, if you are an insurance salesman, it will be in your interest to narrow a prospect's focus from the general goal of selecting an investment to that of providing financial security. What you are suggesting to the prospect, in effect, is to make a quick decision that his broad investment goals would be served best by concentrating on secure areas, and that his primary objective, therefore, is to select the best means of achieving the desired security. Some data on the performance of the stock market, for instance, might be useful in engineering this quick decision in favor of security.

It is generally more difficult to narrow a buyer's

definition of his basic goal than to broaden it since narrowing eliminates possible alternatives. When you are advocating expansion of the buyer's goal definition, you can point out that the buyer incurs no risk by following your suggestion; he merely includes new alternatives without excluding any options that he considered originally.

When you're suggesting a narrowed definition, on the other hand, the change generally must be supported by proof that the original broader focus was not in the buyer's best interests. For instance, the caustic soda salesman in our example had to demonstrate the inferiority of the caustic soda substitutes before he could narrow the buyer's goal definition.

Despite the fact that it is more difficult to narrow a buyer's decision, there are few risks attached to failure. Even if the buyer resists the new definition, the salesman's product is still in the running. For instance, caustic soda is still one means of adjusting the pH, just as insurance is still one form of investment.

In summary, then, a careful definition of the buyer's basic goal can be a key element in the presentation. It is especially important to get the buyer's agreement to a definition that differs from his initial perception, and it is essential to procure such agreement early in the presentation since everything that follows will be based on the new definition. If the buyer seems unwilling to agree to the proposed definition, it may be necessary to halt the presentation and return to fact finding.

Clearly, if the new definition is unacceptable to the prospect, there must have been some early misunderstanding about his primary goals, and the next task must be to clear up that misunderstanding and identify the basic goal more accurately. If you find yourself in this position, you can simply state that you were mistaken and feel you need to do more fact finding. The chances of this happening, however, are slight as long as the altered definition stays in line with the buyer's basic requirements. Generally, getting agreement to a new goal definition is not all that difficult since you are only asking the buyer to look at his decision task in a different way rather than to make a decision at this point. From the buyer's point of view, the risks involved in agreeing to this are negligible.

IDENTIFYING THE BUYER'S CRITERIA

In discussing the structure of the sales presentation, we are following the sequence of the buying decision process. One might question whether it is necessary to stick strictly to this sequence. After all, many successful sales presentations have been made by salesmen who had no understanding of the systematic buying process, who had never thought about the process of making a rational buying decision.

The purpose of the sales presentation is to demonstrate the match between the buyer's ends and the salesman's means, or, in other words, to communicate the logic of selecting your product. A sales presentation that makes it clear that your product or service is matched to the buyer's ends better than any other alternative is likely to be successful, whether or not it follows the sequence defined by the buying decision process. But this sequence provides an organized, orderly way of making your demonstration; it gives structure to the presentation. After all, the buyer is making the decision; what better way is there to arrange a presentation than to move him through each of the critical steps in his decision?

In dealing with the buyer's criteria, the salesman has two choices:

- He can concentrate on identifying the buyer's criteria, summarizing them and seeking agreement on them without any mention of his product.
- He can identify the buyer's criteria and, as he does so, discuss how his product performs against each criterion, whether constraint or objective.

The first approach is useful when the situation is complex, say, when the buyer has a great number of objectives and constraints or when the salesman has many suggestions about the buyer's criteria that he wants him to accept. Another situation in which it is useful to summarize all criteria before proceeding to evaluate your product is in a service sale where the service is designed specifically for the buyer. The criteria in this case serve as the design specifications, and it is important to present them clearly to the buyer so that he can follow the reasoning for the characteristics of the service as it has been designed.

The second approach works well in simple situations, for instance, when the buyer's criteria have not been shaped or the product has not been designed from scratch or altered to fit his requirements. In a straightforward industrial commodities sale, for example, it is certainly possible and advisable to review the buyer's criteria individually and in so doing show how your product meets each criterion.

In the following, we will concentrate on the more complex situation, in which it is advantageous to review the buyer's criteria before evaluating your product.

As indicated earlier, the more the salesman has

shaped the buyer's criteria—his constraints, objectives, and priorities—the more important it is to review them carefully. Your goal here is to get the buyer's agreement to your definition of his criteria. Generally this is not as difficult as it may sound. During earlier stages of the sales process there has been a give and take of information, a gradual understanding and sharpening of the buyer's criteria. At the presentation, then, you are unlikely to surprise the buyer with criteria that haven't been discussed previously. In other words, you're not about to spring completely new ideas on the buyer. Rather, you're trying to restate his criteria in a way that conforms closely to his original perceptions and therefore is likely to be acceptable to him.

Your credibility is another important factor supporting your recommendations. In general, provided the criteria you propose stay within the framework of the buyer's real requirements and you take the time to review each criterion, there should be no difficulty in getting the buyer's agreement. Also, remember that you should try (and indeed should need) to shape only a few buyer criteria. Thus, your review is no more than a restatement of criteria specified, in most cases, by the buyer himself, with the addition of a few criteria that, while altered slightly from their original version, are still recognizable as deriving from the buyer's framework of basic requirements. Even if you suggest new criteria, they will still be recognizable as facets of the buyer's basic, though originally overlooked, needs.

The main point of our discussion is that your review of the buyer's criteria establishes the framework for analyzing your product. Without it, the buyer's perceptions of his own criteria may be unsharp, making it impossible for him to evaluate your product's performance adequately. Unless he sees his objectives clearly, he will not be able to appreciate the degree to which your product achieves them. Your message, then, would be expressed in a statement such as the following:

> "Before we get into an examination of my product, I'd like to review with you the limits that we're working within and the things we are trying to achieve within these limits—your objectives. And then we want to be clear on the priority of these objectives. That way we'll be in a good position to evaluate how well the products meets all our requirements."

With this kind of review, you give your product the maximum opportunity to display its performance, because performance is judged in terms of objectives achieved. Within established limits, the more objectives achieved, the better the product's performance. Clearly, before the buyer can make such an evaluation, he must first have a clear perception of what his objectives are.

IDENTIFYING YOUR PRODUCT

Once you have reviewed with the buyer the criteria on which he will base his decision, the next step is to identify your product. Depending on the nature of the product, this step may be quick and simple or time-consuming and complex. If you're dealing with a product that existed before the sales call, identification tends to be simple. All that is required is a description of the product that will give the buyer a basic understanding of its general properties. When the product or service has been developed especially for the buyer—that is, when it has been designed from scratch or substantially redesigned—you may need to spend more time on this step. An architect, for instance, would have to present drawings of a proposed building developed specifically for a particular buyer. Similarly, an investment counselor may need to go into some detail to describe the elements of an investment program he has developed for a potential client.

How detailed this identification step is, then, depends largely on the degree of the buyer's knowledge of the product and/or the general product area. A buyer of industrial chemicals probably will not need a lengthy description of a product that is similar to those which he buys customarily. By contrast, a potential client of an architect is in need of information about the particular design the architect is offering, because he is utterly unfamiliar with it.

What is needed is a product description that demonstrates how your product meets the buyer's criteria. In other words, the identification of your product is really an introduction that provides the basis for a detailed evaluation of the product in terms of the buyer's criteria. The buyer, as we've seen, is interested not in the product per se but in its ability to achieve his specific ends.

The product-oriented salesman typically mistakes this act of describing his product for that of presenting it—indeed, for the act of selling. Product-oriented salesmen tend to rely heavily on brochures and other such prepackaged descriptions, in the belief that these glossy aids support their verbal description, making it more exciting and thereby improving the chances of a sale. But an impersonal, generalized description of a product does not answer the real question in the buyer's mind: "How does this product achieve *my individual* needs, goals, and requirements?" Because such standardized presentations rely on the buyer to figure out how his individual needs might be met by the salesman's product, the control over the situation is entirely in the buyer's hands The product-oriented salesman, in other words, has no real impact on the buyer's decision.

The customer-oriented salesman, on the other hand, realizes that this step in the presentation is less important than the following evaluation of his product's performance against the buyer's specific criteria. He may still use brochures and other descriptive aids, but he doesn't confuse the act of passing them out with the act of making a presentation.

EVALUATING THE PRODUCT IN TERMS
OF THE BUYER'S CRITERIA

As we have said, the key element in the presentation is the evaluation of your product in terms of the buyer's individual decision criteria. We have also made the point that the salesman should follow exactly the sequence of steps in the buying-decision process. In particular, during evaluation he should first demonstrate that his product meets the buyer's constraints, next that there are no unacceptable risks attached to it, and finally that it meets each of the buyer's objectives.

This is a logical path to follow. Still, there may be salesmen who, because of their individual style or a unique situation, want to rearrange the sequence of these steps. Will this turn the presentation into a failure? Probably not. In fact, it may sometimes be advisable to hold off discussion of a particular constraint until the end of the evaluation phase. The cost of your product, for example, must obviously fall within the buyer's budget constraint, but you may wish to deal with it as late as possible. You may, therefore, deal with certain other constraints and prove your product's acceptability in those respects.

Next, you might move to a demonstration that there are no significant risks attached to your product. Then you might want to analyze how the product meets the buyer's objectives, to turn to the question of cost only at the end. The price of your product, for example, might just meet the buyer's limits, and therefore you would want to build your case for your product before discussing the price question. Obviously, you need to deal with the buyer's price constraint at some point, but you needn't feel compelled to cover it first, and at times you may indeed be wiser not to.

The important point, however, is that during your presentation, all of the buyer's evaluation must be covered—his constraints, risks, the objectives, and priorities. It is not crucial that they be covered in that order as long as they are all covered at some point during the evaluation phase of the presentation.

Meeting the Buyer's Constraints

A constraint, as we have seen, is an inflexible limit. During the fact-finding stage and the first part of the presentation the salesman and the buyer have come to an agreement about these limits. The task now becomes to supply proof that the salesman's product falls within them. Generally, this is a simple yes-or-no situation: A product either meets the buyer's constraints or it doesn't. And since these constraints generally deal with measurable resources like money, space, or time, this part of the presentation usually is straightforward:

"Yes, our storage tank will fit in the space set aside for such a tank, and here are the dimensions."

Or:

"Yes, our mill can produce 100 units per hour, and here are the specifications and the results of other users."

The technique is simple: identify the buyer's constraints and supply proof (in whatever detail is necessary) to document the fact that your product falls within the limits established by the buyer.

It is here, in dealing with the buyer's constraints, that much of your product knowledge comes into play. Here is where you need the technical information, all the various specifications of your product, because such proof data are critical as basis for supporting your statements. Unfortunately, however, in their sales training programs, many companies spend much, even most, of their time teaching this kind of product knowledge. Ironically, the result is often a group of product-oriented salesmen, people who know all about the product but nothing about how to sell it, that is, how to develop buying decisions. There are two aspects to product knowledge: understanding what the product is all about and—just as importantly—knowing how to use that information in the sales process.

Evaluating Risks

A perceived risk, like a constraint, can cause the buyer to eliminate a product from further consideration. In the presentation, you should therefore take care to prove to the buyer that there are no unacceptable risks attached to your product. You should satisfy him, in other words, that if he selects your product, there will be no nasty surprises awaiting him down the road.

Of course, buyers don't always consider risks carefully. Nonetheless, you are wise to assume that the prospect will worry about risks at some point in his deliberations, and you should deal with the problem early in the presentation in order to get it out of the way. You are interested in two kinds of risks: those the buyer himself has identified and is concerned about and those which could become a factor later as he considers his decision in detail. Your goal is to eliminate both kinds of concerns by proving that the risks involved are nonexistent, so negligible as to be meaningless, or, at the very least, acceptable.

Even in a situation in which there is a genuine but acceptable risk attached to your product, it is in your interest to discuss it with the buyer; to gloss over it is to sow potential service problems after the sale is made. You win little if you create a potentially dissatisfied customer. As we have seen, dissatisfaction is a powerful motive for considering a new purchase—most probably not from you but from the competition. On the other hand, if you draw the buyer's attention to possible risks attached to your product and later these risks materialize, he will have made an informed decision and will be less likely to blame you as the salesman who engineered it.

In short, you must deal with risks in the presentation. This is not to say that if you have an essentially risk-free product you should go out of your way to find out risks, but only that you should deal openly with significant risks, if there are any, and help the buyer evaluate their extent.

Once again, product data are important here. If you're selling nuclear reactors, you inevitably must deal with the question of potential radioactive leaks. The question that you have to answer, in this case, is how real the risk of such leaks is. Information about the design of the reactor, its construction specifications and safety features clearly would play a critical role in demonstrating that the risks involved are negligible and do not warrant dropping the product from further consideration.

Of course, what is an unacceptable risk to one buyer might be perfectly acceptable to another. The salesman's task, therefore, is to present the kind of product data that answer stated and potential worries of the buyer. Since there are no hard and fast rules about what is "acceptable," the more data the salesman can supply in support of his contentions, the better his chances of influencing the buyer's judgment.

Discussing the risks facing a buyer can also give you a competitive edge. Often you know who your competitors are, and you have a pretty good idea of their products and how they perform compared to yours. In such a situation, it is certainly feasible to discuss the competitor's products with the buyer and to demonstrate what risks they carry.

To a large extent, this is a question of style. Many salesmen and buyers follow the philosophy that it is bad form to knock the competition. In general, this is probably a good rule. But "knocking the competition" is not the same as pointing out to the buyer that he should consider the risks involved in each of the alternatives he is considering. In this latter case, you are only consistent with your customer-oriented approach to selling: You are helping the buyer make a quality buying decision, which presupposes evaluating all risks. Just as it is in yours and the buyer's interest to evaluate risks attached to your product, so it is in both your interests to examine risks that come with the competitors' products.

If you gain a competitive edge by initiating this evaluation, then so be it; it really is inherent in the comparison between the competing products. Your job is to exploit this edge by bringing it to the buyer's attention. Not to do so would be to miss a legitimate opportunity, apart from allowing the buyer to choose a product without prior consideration of the potential negative consequences.

You must exercise good judgment here. Whether to discuss the potential risks attached to your product and/or to those of your competitors depends on how real they are to the *prospect*. A quality buying decision demands that the buyer consider genuine risks; it does not require him to worry about trivialities.

One final point: Often you can cause a buyer to consider risks attached to a competing product simply by introducing certain objectives that you believe that buyer has. In making your presentation for a chemicals storage tank, for example, you might broach the subject of tank linings and mention relevant risks:

> "In considering your alternatives you should also be sure that the storage tank which you select has a heavy-duty lining. Leaks caused by thin linings can mean violations of OSHA regulations, which in turn could shut your plant down for a time."

The buyer may not even have considered tank linings, but by introducing this risk in the context of his objectives, in particular, his desire for continuous plant operation, you are bringing the question of leaks to the buyer's attention, and in so doing, you may well gain an edge over your competitors—and without even mentioning them. When confronted with this question, your competitor's salesman's job, of course, is to supply data proving that the risks of leaks with thinner linings is nonexistent or negligible.

Evaluating Your Product against the Buyer's Objectives

If there is any idea on which all salesmen agree, it is that you've got to sell "benefits." Benefits are to selling what motherhood and apple pie are to American culture.

In the introduction to this chapter we discussed

the importance of approaching the presentation as a communications task. Your goal in this phase is to convey to the buyer the logic of selecting your particular product. To put it differently, the presentation is designed to communicate to the prospect the benefits that your product will create for him. These benefits, as we've seen, are relative to the buyer's needs. A fur-lined parka may provide benefits to an Eskimo, but it is utterly useless to a nomad in the Sahara.

While this may seem perfectly reasonable, the fact is that most salesmen do not sell as though benefits were relative, but as if they were absolute, inherent in the product and independent of the buyer's needs. This is what characterizes product-oriented selling, in which the salesman describes the various "benefits" of his product regardless of whether the buyer cares about them or not.

Faced with the product-oriented salesman's presentation, the buyer uses the salesman's description of his product as a source of general information. Sifting through his personal criteria, he sees if they are in any degree met by the product *as he perceives it,* and based on that evaluation, he makes his choice. But the salesman has not affected the buyer's perception of the product's utility, because he has failed to demonstrate clearly how his product meets each of the buyer's criteria.

All this is neglected by the feature/benefit approach and left to the buyer to analyze. The product-oriented salesman is no more than a spokesman for his product—a medium for information. This explains in part why there is such a heavy emphasis on "closing" in feature/benefit selling. A sale is "closed" when the buyer decides to buy. If the salesman does not work with the buyer to *develop* his buying decision, then he must somehow *extract* that decision. Whereas in a customer-oriented approach to selling, the buyer's decision results from a logical process in which buyer and seller work together to select the best alternative, given the buyer's criteria, the feature/benefit decision is often unrelated to the efforts of the salesman, whose only contribution to the process is a description of the product.

The feature/benefit salesman must rely on persuasion techniques to close the sale. This in turn has led to sales training emphasizing behavioral psychology. An effective salesman, under this philosophy, is seen as someone who can articulate a smooth product description and manipulate the buyer's behavior so as to motivate him to buy.

"Persuasive" selling, then, involves a product description followed by a compelling close. The close is regarded as the climax of the sale. In customer-oriented selling, on the other hand, the close is the least important event, in terms of its demands on the salesman's energies; it is but the logical result of the efforts that preceded it—the analysis, the strategy, the presentation—all of which were designed to uncover the buyer's requirements before demonstrating how they are met by the product.

Does this mean that there is no place for feature/benefit type selling? Are straight product descriptions never useful? And what's wrong with "dynamic" presentations? Shouldn't there be some *excitement* in the presentation—and in the product?

Of course, all of these things have their place. Excitement and glitter are often necessary commodities in a sales presentation. Slick packages, both of the product and the presentation, are often useful and important. The key point is to know when and where to employ these devices, to understand their limitations.

Feature/benefit selling is essentially *product description* that is unrelated to the particular buyer's criteria. It is useful, therefore, in two kinds of situations in marketing, where it is impossible to individualize the message because of the audience (for instance, in a television commercial); and at the *beginning* of a sales interview when a buyer is unfamiliar with the product area. In the second case, a feature/benefit product description can be helpful to the buyer in developing his personal criteria for the product. One way of determining one's objectives with regard to a specific product area, for example, is to look at the available alternatives. If you're thinking about buying a horse, yet know nothing about it, one way to start developing your criteria for the ultimate decision is to get exposure by examining a number of animals and talking to breeders.

For the salesman, the key point is not to confuse a feature/benefit description with the sales process but to recognize it as just one way to begin the process. Your work properly starts when you sit down with the buyer to develop his individual criteria. Only then can the salesman make a presentation.

It's possible, then, to think of a feature/benefit presentation as a way of starting the sales process, even of *motivating* the buyer to begin the process. The excitement of a product description in a television commercial is designed, after all, to arouse your sense of the opportunity to be gained by investigating the advertised product. When we are dealing with complex products such as industrial equipment or financial services, however, the effect of the advertisement will not go beyond this motivation step; it still requires the professional efforts of the local salesman to develop your buying decision.

There's one final point to be made about feature/ benefit selling. Proponents of this approach place as much emphasis on "answering objections" as on closing techniques. The classic objection occurs in the form of indifference to a particular feature or benefit extolled by the salesman. "Who cares?" the buyer might respond, or: "I'm not interested in that." In a customer-oriented presentation, there is much less likelihood of this kind of buyer objection, because the product is presented from the perspective of the buyer's individual criteria, and he is certainly not indifferent to his own previously stated objectives. The only question on his mind is how well your product meets his objectives.

We have seen, then, that selling benefits must not be confused with giving a generalized product description. Your task at this point is to demonstrate the utility of the product from the perspective of the buyer's individual objectives. This is a matter of examining each objective, showing to what degree your product meets it, and supplying whatever data are necessary to document your claims.

In doing this, it is best to start with the buyer's top priority objective and work your way down the list, demonstrating for each objective how well the product meets it. Remember that decisions are compromises. The buyer will rarely achieve everything he had in mind. This is true for his overall list of objectives (while he may achieve some of them completely, there may be others that he doesn't achieve at all) as well as for his individual objectives (that is, many of them he may not be able to achieve completely). Thus, your task often is to demonstrate that your product, while not perfect, still is his *best* choice, namely the one that meets his important objectives better than any other alternative.

As we have seen, when the buyer considers his constraints and evaluates risks, he makes absolute judgments: A product either meets a constraint or it doesn't. With objectives, on the other hand, there is no absolute. If a buyer's objective in buying a car is to get 40 miles per gallon, the *perfect* choice is a model that gets 40 mpg. But if none of the available products provides that kind of mileage, the *best* performer obviously is the one that comes closest to the buyer's objective. In general, the buyer's best choice is the product that outperforms the others in more of his *high-priority* objectives.

The moral of this is that you should not be dismayed if your product is not the perfect choice. Your task in the presentation is to demonstrate not perfection but superiority. This doesn't mean that you must compare your product's performance with that of your competitors' (although that option is certainly open to you) but only that you must concentrate on each of the buyers' objectives and provide whatever data are necessary to document your product's ability to meet it.

In summary, then, evaluating the product's performance is the step in the presentation that is concerned with proving "benefits." Since benefits are relative—that is, exist to the degree to which a product meets the buyer's objectives—proving them requires you to present data about product performance for each buyer objective. The more completely the product meets the full range of objectives, the better a choice it is, and the more data you can supply to document performance against each objective, the more clearly the buyer will *perceive* the benefits provided by your product. And perceived value is the only value that counts.

IDENTIFYING ADDITIONAL BENEFITS

Up to this point in the presentation you have:

Restated the buyer's motive for considering a purchase.

Defined his basic goal.

Summarized his criteria.

Identified your product.

Proved that your product meets the buyer's constraints.

Proved that it carries no unacceptable risks.

Evaluated its performance against each of the buyer's objectives.

According to our model of the buying-decision process, the prospect should now be in a position to decide; he should clearly perceive that your product represents his best choice. In many cases, the buyer will indeed be ready at this point to make the decision. All his concerns have been identified and analyzed, and you've taken him step by step through a systematic evaluation process.

There is an opportunity here, however, to strengthen the buyer's commitment to your product by demonstrating some "additional benefits." These are benefits associated with your product that are outside the buyer's original decision framework but may be attractive to him as a kind of bonus. He could certainly live without them since he has not even thought of them. (Had he done so, they would have been represented in his original list of criteria.) Still, once his attention is directed at them, they may represent an additional attraction.

Pointing out additional benefits is *not* a matter of reciting the whole catalogue of features and benefits of your product. To do so at this stage of the sales process would be to blur the carefully constructed steps in the buyer's decision.

For example, an advertising space salesman would concentrate in his presentation on the magazine's ability to achieve the marketing or communication objectives of the client. The advertiser, for his part, will make his decision based on how well the magazine can reach an audience of specific size and description. Once the salesman has demonstrated his magazine's performance with regard to these specific objectives, he may want to mention some selected additional benefits of advertising in his magazine, say, a special service that the magazine supplies to its advertisers.

Suppose, for instance, that the magazine is willing to provide the advertiser's sales force with sales training in particular aspects of the market that the magazine reaches. Sales training, or the effectiveness of his sales force, is clearly a concern of the advertiser—though not the kind that he would bring to his *advertising* decision. It is not the kind of objective, in other words, that the salesman could logically suggest as he and the buyer are working together to develop the decision criteria. Still, sales training is an additional benefit that the salesman's product can deliver, and it might just be the factor that solidifies the buyer's commitment. More likely it will simply make him happier with a decision he would have made anyway.

In general, then, mentioning additional benefits can only enhance your presentation as long as you realize when and where they apply. They are strictly secondary, and you should try to construct the buyer's decision in a way that makes additional benefits unnecessary to a successful sale.

Another source of "additional benefits" is found in the possible consequences of a purchase. Just as the salesman and the buyer considered the risks the buyer is running if he selects a certain product, it is possible to discuss potential positive results of choosing it. In a sense, they are the opposite of risks, namely desirable things that *might* happen if the product is bought. Such results obviously go beyond the buyer's expectations of the product's performance. All he can reasonably expect is for the product to meet his objectives, but, in some cases, there is a chance that it will create certain beneficial side effects. The chemicals salesman selling a liquid product that competes with dry powders might tell the buyer that some users have noticed better labor performance because of improved working conditions. While there is no guarantee that this will happen, there is at least a chance of such improvement, which would represent an attractive side benefit of purchasing the liquid product.

Again, secondary benefits by definition play a peripheral role in the buying decision process. To give them too much attention means to place your emphasis incorrectly and potentially confuse the crucial aspects of the decision. Not to mention them at all, on the other hand, is possibly to overlook additional opportunities to influence the buyer's decision in favor of your product.

HANDLING OBJECTIONS

No analysis of the sales process is complete without some mention of objections.

When a prospective customer objects, it generally is because he disagrees with some of your statements about a product's utility, its value, the benefits it provides. As we discussed earlier, this kind of objection is quite common in a feature/benefit sale because the buyer is forced to sit through an exposition of a

number of product features that may be totally irrelevant to him. Predictably, when the salesman pro-
ceeds to proclaim the benefits to be gained from these
features, the buyer reacts with objections, stating that
he isn't interested in some of the alleged benefits. The
salesman is then forced to try to overcome the objections by whatever means.

In a customer-oriented sales approach, these kinds
of objections are rare. Since the salesman presents his
product in the light of the buyer's own criteria, he
should not run into buyer objections concerning the
relevance of a particular point or "feature."

This is not to say, of course, that the customer-
oriented salesman never encounters resistance or objections. There are two basic kinds of objections that
you may experience:

- A specific objection disputing the product's performance against a particular criterion.
- A general objection doubting the overall performance of the product without any specific or
  clearly defined reason—a general reluctance to
  make the decision.

In the case of a specific objection you can rely on
your data about product performance to dispel the
customer's doubts. Of course, if you have developed
your presentation thoroughly, the chances of this kind
of objection are greatly reduced because you will already have supplied all available data to back up your
contentions about the product's ability to meet the
buyer's objectives. It clearly is best to anticipate potential objections and to forestall them by presenting
the appropriate data.

The more substantial your proof data, furthermore,
the more difficult the buyer will find it to object. This
suggests strongly that the more clear-cut the objective,

the more precisely *measurable* it is, the easier it is for you to supply supporting data about your product's ability to meet it, which in turn decreases the chances that the prospect will be able to raise legitimate objections. Compare, for instance, the two objectives "good gas mileage" and "38 miles per gallon." In making your sales presentation, it is clearly easier to provide precise performance information on the "38 miles per gallon" objective than on the more general one, and hence there will be less room for buyer objections in the first case.

Unfortunately, it is not always possible to develop such precise buyer objectives. In some cases it is not even in the salesman's interest to do so. If you're selling big cars getting no more than 15 miles per gallon, you clearly would be better off with a general "good mileage" objective than with one demanding 38 miles per gallon. Nonetheless, our basic principle remains valid. Objections arise because of doubt about a product's ability to meet certain objectives. This type of objection must be met by presenting precise performance data, and the more measurable the objectives, the easier it is to supply the pertinent data.

In the case of more general objections that express doubts about the decision as a whole, two points should be noted. First, one of the main advantages of a customer-oriented approach to selling is that it tends to reduce the possibility of such vague, general objections, which are generally caused by poor decision making. This kind of objection is most common in a feature/benefit approach. The buyer, having looked at the product, is not sure whether it perhaps holds some unpleasant surprises. The reason for his doubts is that he has not taken the time to examine his own criteria. He has not established the constraints he must observe, nor has he identified precisely what he is trying to achieve as a result of the purchase. He is in no position, therefore, to make a good evaluation of the products available. He may listen to the salesman's description of various product features and benefits, but in the end he still has doubts that are translated into the kinds of general objections which frustrate many a salesman.

If you concentrate from the beginning on developing the buyer's criteria *with* him, you are much less likely to run into this problem during your presentation. The whole point of our approach is to make explicit all of the buyer's criteria and use them to evaluate your product. When the buyer and you have completed the process of developing his buying decision, the buyer knows his limits, his objectives, his priorities, the risks he is facing, and the performance of your product in the areas important to him; he even knows in which areas he will have to compromise. He should clearly see that your product is the best means to achieve his ends. The chances are, therefore, that general objections will not arise.

Still, doubts may arise, and this leads to our second point concerning general objections. If, at the end of the presentation, the buyer gives evidence of reluctance to make up his mind, raising vague objections, this must be taken as an indication that something important has been overlooked in the sales process. Perhaps an objective or constraint has been missed; perhaps the buyer's priorities have been analyzed incorrectly. When faced with this kind of objection, you therefore should confront the buyer with your belief that both he and you have missed some important information about the buyer's requirements. The task then becomes to go back over the buyer's criteria to adjust them or add new ones.

The essential point is to keep the emphasis on the

buyer's criteria rather than on your product. You do not want to place yourself in the position of having to defend the product against vague objections. Instead, you should stay firmly with your customer-oriented approach and find out what additional ends the buyer has in mind so that you can, if necessary, redesign the means to achieve them. Just as there are no inherent benefits in a product, there are no inherent deficiencies. The quality of the product—its usefulness or lack of it—is determined by its ability to meet the individual buyer's requirements. Hence the best strategy is not to defend your product but rather to reexamine the buyer's criteria in order to determine how the match between ends and means can be improved.

CLOSING THE SALE

The "close" is nothing but the logical result of the systematic process preceding it. This implies that it is, or should be, anticlimactic. The decision process that the salesman has developed with the buyer is a logical series of steps that starts from a great mass of information and, in analyzing it, gradually reduces the buyer's options until just one alternative is left: his best choice. Less effective alternatives fall by the wayside at some point in the process. The close, then, is the agreement that the product is indeed the buyer's best choice, and that agreement, being the result of a number of prior judgments and evaluations, is the natural conclusion of the entire process. If the buyer reaches this point and still feels reluctant to commit himself to the decision, you are faced with an "objection" situation, which you handle as we have already discussed. If there are no objections, your next step is to establish procedures for implementing the decision. This can involve any number of tasks from arranging for product delivery to scheduling additional meetings in order to sign contracts or develop further implementation plans. All these details obviously depend on the product and the situation and need not concern us here.

In summary, then, the close is really the last of a series of closes, or agreements between you and the buyer as you moved through the decision-making process. Far from being a final grand climax, it is a last logical note in a careful design.

THE PRESENTATION IN SUMMARY

It will be useful at this point to recapitulate briefly the basic steps in the presentation. They are as follows:

- Restating the buyer's original motive for entering the decision process.
- Defining his basic goal.
- Reviewing his evaluation criteria, starting with his constraints and proceeding to his objectives and priorities.
- Identifying your product.
- Proving the product's ability to meet the buyer's constraints.
- Evaluating risks attached to various alternatives.
- Evaluating your product's performance with respect to the buyer's objectives and supplying data to prove your claims.
- Identifying additional benefits that may be important to the buyer.
- Answering objections, either specific or general.
- Closing the sale, that is, establishing plans to implement the buying decision.

These steps represent the basic structure for any presentation. Their sequence follows that defined by our model of the systematic buying decision, and it must do so because in the presentation, the salesman is in fact constructing the buyer's decision for him.

THE MEDIUM OF THE MESSAGE

At the beginning of this chapter we emphasized the importance of good communications in sales. The more complex the sales situation, the more important it is that the salesman communicate effectively. We then discussed how using the decision process as a model for the presentation improves the communication between salesman and buyer because it provides the structure around which the salesman can organize all relevant information about the buyer's requirements and the product's performance. This will allow the buyer to see clearly the match between his ends and the means—your product. The decision model, in other words, facilitates communication by providing a logical organization of the message the salesman is trying to convey.

Besides the message, however, there is another aspect to communication: the medium, the means by which the message is conveyed. Basically, you have three kinds of media available for your presentation: spoken, written, and audiovisual.

The vast majority of the time you will use the oral medium. There are times, however, when you should consider employing other media to assist your oral presentation. The major drawback to an oral presentation is its transitoriness. Once it is made, it disappears. If the buyer reaches the decision at the end of the presentation, this doesn't matter; your presentation has served its purpose, and there is no earthly reason to preserve it for history. Sometimes, however, this impermanence is a serious weakness.

For example, in a complex sale there are often several people involved in the buying decision. In those cases you may be able to assemble all of the decision makers into one room and make your presentation orally. More commonly, you must deal with only one or two of them, and these people will subsequently make a recommendation to their management, which then makes the final decision, often without having had significant contact with you. In such situations, the transitoriness of the oral medium becomes a very real problem for you. You may have made the most well-reasoned presentation possible, and at the time, the people you dealt with may have seen the logic of selecting your product and may have been ready and willing to make a positive recommendation. When the time comes for them to justify their recommendation, however, it is unlikely that they will be able to reconstruct your presentation as effectively as you could. Their management—the ultimate decision makers—will therefore not have the full benefit of your original presentation, and hence the logic of the buying decision will not be as apparent to them. If this happens, you run the risk of losing the sale.

In such a case you must supply the "recommender" with a detailed *written* proposal containing the same message as your oral presentation. This will give him the material he needs to reconstruct the decision. In all probability, this proposal will simply be passed on to top management with the recommender's positive comments. Not only is the logic of your presentation kept intact through all levels of the subsequent decision process, but by supplying the recommender with a well-reasoned and detailed analysis of the buying decision, you are doing him a genuine service because you're giving him a chance to present his superiors with a well-documented explanation of his decision, demonstrably based on his company's own constraints, objectives, and priorities. In short, you're helping him demonstrate his own competence and thoroughness. Clearly, it can never hurt you to afford a buyer such professional aid.

The key point is that you cannot rely on buyers to reconstruct your oral presentation. In cases of multiple decision makers, therefore, a written proposal must accompany any oral presentation. That proposal should contain the same message—the same details organized in the same fashion—as your oral presentation so that the careful reasoning for the buying decision is kept intact as your product is considered at various levels of the buyer's organization.

There are times, furthermore, when your presentation would benefit from the use of audiovisual media such as flip charts, slides, films, or videotape. At the lower end of the scale, flip charts can be useful to augment an oral presentation by highlighting certain key aspects of the presentation. The more sophisticated media—slides, film, and videotape—are useful when the salesman wants to generate excitement in his buyers. Audiovisual media are *affective.* They can arouse an emotional response not directly related to the more rational decision-making processes. The uses of film and videotape for propaganda and for advertising demonstrate the power of these media. Their influence on the individual, however, is short-lived, and hence the secret of any effective advertising or propaganda campaign is repetition. A one-shot television advertisement is generally non-productive.

This is an important indication of the limitation of audiovisual media. You cannot rely on their effects to develop a decision and to maintain commitment to it. Audiovisual media speak mainly to the senses and to the emotions, and these are not the faculties involved in good decision making. Still, these media can be useful in adding excitement to the sales process, as long as the essential elements of the buying decision are not blurred.

These considerations may be helpful to the salesman and the sales organization in considering whether and when to use audiovisual media to support the sales effort. These media can be very useful at the start of a presentation, where they help remotivate the buyer, say, by quantifying the opportunity that the product or service offers him. Media can also support the body of the presentation. Again, the salesman's basic message is unchanged: He is reconstructing the buyer's decision in order to demonstrate the logic of selecting his product. But audiovisual aids can support and augment this message by adding affective qualities inherent in the medium.

Are we then contradicting the basic premises of this book? Does the suggestion that salesmen use *affective* media in the presentation contradict our concern for logic and careful analysis of buying decisions, our emphasis on developing quality decisions that lead to repeat sales? Are we, after all, reverting to pizzazz? No! Salesmen and sales organizations run into problems when they try to mix excitement with their message and in so doing gloss over the decision process. Feature/benefit approaches to selling commonly try to build affective values into the message. What we are suggesting is that the presentation message remains untouched; its essence is aimed at a well-reasoned buying decision. The excitement, the affective values, reside in the medium, not the message, and can be added without detracting from the logical quality of your sales message.

When should you use these audiovisual media? Basically, this is a question of economy. Audiovisuals are expensive to produce, and your decision comes down to evaluating the cost/benefit ratio. Is the ultimate sale worth the cost of producing audiovisuals in order to support the presentation? Will the addition of audiovisual media substantially enhance the possibility of making the sale, for instance by increasing the credibility and stature of the salesman or organization? Can you produce general audiovisuals that will work in a number of sales situations, thereby spreading the cost and reducing the risk? These questions cannot be answered here. The point to remember is that audiovisuals by themselves cannot *sell* any complex product; they cannot develop buying decisions. The message, the reconstruction of the buyer's decision in the presentation is what sells, because selling is engineering quality buying decisions.

One final point about audiovisual media: They provide for consistency, for the content of such programs is invariable. In this they differ from salesmen who will say different things at different times in different ways even when describing the same product. Thus, when a standard product description is called for, an audiovisual program may be useful. As we've said, however, packaged product descriptions, like feature/benefit presentations, are severely limited in their usefulness. The key to systematic selling is matching the product to the individual buyer's ends and presenting it in that perspective. Standardized product descriptions by definition cannot provide the required specificity and therefore are useful only to support the salesman's individualized presentation.

In short, the medium won't sell the product, but only the salesman who takes the trouble to understand the buyer's decision problem and presents his product as a logical response to the buyer's needs. The message, not the medium, is the essence of systematic selling.

INDEX

prospect (cont.)
knowledge of basic motives
and goal of, 75–77
old customers as, 69
questions asked of, 89–90, 93
referrals and, 71–72
servicing of, 71
technique of developing,
67–73

questioning
of prospect, 89–90, 93
skill in, 86–87

real estate, buyer's criteria in,
118–121, 123
referrals, prospects from, 71–72
relevant facts, finding of,
85–107
see also information
risk
in buyer decision, 100
unacceptable, 40–41
risk evaluation, 23–24
in sales presentation, 162–
165

sales
"human skills" in, 84
vs. marketing, 131–132
opening of, 74–85
see also opening
sales-expansive service, 63–64
sales interview
basic questions to ask in, 88
prior knowledge in, 75–76
see also opening; sales presentation
salesman
credibility of, 157
customer-oriented, 48, 114,
160
listening by, 86–87

product knowledge of, 120
product-oriented, 85, 114,
159–160, 166
prospect and, 68–69
sales presentation, 146–184
"additional benefits" ap-
proach in, 171–173
audiovisual media in, 181–
184
basic goal definition in,
150–155
"benefits" in, 166–173
buyer's criteria in, 155–158
"closing the sale" in, 177–
178
feature/benefit selling in,
166–171
handling objections in, 173–
177
medium of message in, 179–
184
motivation of buyer in, 147–
150
product identification in,
158–160
risk evaluation in, 162–165
summary of, 178–179
written proposal in, 180–181
sales process, basic steps in, 49,
108
sales strategy, 108–145
basic steps in, 49, 108
"closing" in, 58–59, 90–91,
177–178
development of, 55–57
illustration of, 132–139
implementation of, 110
presentation and, *see* sales
presentation
product redesign and, 109–
110
in sales presentation, 146